The American Fiddle Method
The Fun Way to Learn Fiddling!

VOL. 2 PIANO Accompaniment

Intermediate Tunes and Techniques

by Brian Wicklund and Bob Walser

Piano Accompaniment for:
American Fiddle Method, Vol. 2 - Fiddle   (MB99472BCD)
and other instruments

1 2 3 4 5 6 7 8 9 0

GRANGER MUSIC PUBLICATIONS, INC.
COPYRIGHT © 2008 BY BRIAN WICKLUND
MEL BAY PUBLICATIONS, INC. (EXCLUSIVE SALES AGENT), PACIFIC, MO 63069.
ALL RIGHTS RESERVED. INTERNATIONAL COPYRIGHT SECURED. B.M.I. MADE AND PRINTED IN U.S.A.
No part of this publication may be reproduced in whole or in part, or stored in a retrieval system, or transmitted in any form
or by any means, electronic, mechanical, photocopy, recording, or otherwise, without written permission of the publisher.

Visit us on the Web at www.melbay.com — E-mail us at email@melbay.com

About the Authors

When Brian Wicklund was seven years old, his mother thought he should take Suzuki violin lessons. He was surprised to find out that he liked it. When he heard fiddle music for the first time as a third-grader, however, he really flipped out. Brian practiced hard and got to be pretty good. As a pimply teen, he won a bunch of fiddle contests and played fiddle, mandolin and guitar in a number of bluegrass bands. After graduating from Gustavus Adolphus College with a degree in elementary education, Brian realized that school teachers have to get up pretty early in the morning and so he joined the internationally known bluegrass band Stoney Lonesome and played with them for seven years. Brian currently keeps a busy schedule teaching lessons and workshops. He is a sought-after studio musician and regularly performs with an array of bluegrass, country, and swing ensembles including Acoustic Power Trio "Brother Mule." His recordings have been given wide critical acclaim. He is a co-founder of bluegrasscollege.org. Find out more about Brian's recordings, performances and workshops at *www.brianwicklund.com*.

Bob Walser will never forget the first night he heard fiddle music: he danced holes through a brand new pair of socks! A few weeks later, Tim Woodbridge showed him how to play simple oom-pah piano in the key of D and let him play at an old time dance in western Massachusetts. Since that fateful night he's played for dances in New England, Olde England and across America with Yankee, Appalachian, Irish, Scottish, English, and French-Canadian fiddlers. Some 30 years later Bob still claims that playing for dancers is his greatest musical thrill. He tries not to let his education training in Orff Schulwerk, and Ph.D. in ethnomusicology get in the way - mostly, he just loves to play! Find out more about Bob at *www.bobandjulie.net*.

About the Illustrator

Brian Barber is pretty tall and has been illustrating and designing for many publications and advertising in Minneapolis since 1989. He moved to Minneapolis from Nebraska, where he attended the University of Nebraska-Lincoln. His musical experience includes playing drums and guitar in several rock and roll bands. His only previous experience with the fiddle was when he was fighting with his sister as a kid and broke her violin bow, and got in really big trouble. Brian's other illustrations are at *www.brianbarber.com*.

Table of Contents

Foreword 4

	Intermediate Tunes	Fiddle Pages	Piano Accomp. Pages
1	Eighth of January	11	5
2	Liberty	12	6
3	St. Anne's Reel	13	8
4	Spotted Pony	14	10
5	Cuckoo's Nest	15	12
6	Old Joe Clark	16	14
7	Soldier's Joy	17	16
8	Swallowtail Jig	18	18
9	June Apple	19	20
10	Fisher's Hornpipe	20	22
11	Liza Jane	21	24
12	Arkansas Traveler	22	26
13	Devil's Dream	23	28
14	Westphalia Waltz	24	30
15	Ragtime Annie	26	34
16	Golden Anniversary Waltz	27	36
17	Big John McNeil	28	38
18	Star of the County Down	30	40
19	Benny's Favorite	31	44
20	Marie Clark	32	46
21	Bernard the Butterfly	34	48
22	Flop-Eared Mule	35	50
23	Swampwalk	36	52
24	Don't Come Home, Johnny	37	54
25	Forked Deer	38	56
26	Jolie Blonde	39	58
27	Big Walleye Blues	40	60

Piano Backup Basics 67
    St. Anne's Reel Variation Example 68

A Guide to Bluegrass Style Arranging **70**

Foreword

It's been some years now since *The American Fiddle Method* was first published. It has grown to become the most widely used fiddle method book in the country. I travel nationwide and will land in a new city to find, to my astonishment, legions of fiddlers playing repertoire from my books. The tunes are being played in school orchestras, jam sessions, bluegrass festivals, and fiddle contests. The fiddlers are jamming with mandolin, banjo, guitar and bass players. They are having so much fun.

However, some folks in violin studios have told me that there is a need for piano accompaniment books for my series. There often isn't someone who can play guitar in their community. Piano-playing teachers, parents, and siblings are much more common and they have been feeling left out of the action. Therefore I called upon my good friend Bob Walser to assist in arranging piano accompaniment books to complement Volumes 1 and 2 of the fiddle series. He was a natural choice. His home is the frequent site of jam sessions in Minneapolis. Many times I have played fiddle in sessions with Bob playing piano or guitar. His choice of harmony and his rhythmic drive always makes playing with him a treat. He's spent his lifetime studying folk music both informally and formally (he has a Ph.D. in ethnomusicology). Working with Bob on this project has been a lot of fun.

Bob and I talked at length about the scope of this book. Piano accompaniment for fiddle tunes can range from the simplest harmonies with a "boom, chuck, boom, chuck" rhythm, to very syncopated jazz re-harmonizing. I felt it important to use the same chords that are written in the fiddle book, but gave Bob leeway to add some fun variations of rhythm and harmony. Also Bob offers a single page of text to succinctly explain the basic concepts of accompanying fiddlers. It's our belief that if you play the arrangements in this book, you'll get a pretty good feeling for the style and will be able to apply the same techniques to other tunes. You will also have all of the fundamentals you need to explore more complex backup concepts.

I am hoping that this book will help spawn new jam sessions where ever there is a fiddle and a piano. Fiddle music is a blast to play and it is Bob's and my pleasure to welcome pianists to the party.

Keep in touch with us.

Brian Wicklund
www.brianwicklund.com

Bob Walser
www.bobandjulie.net

1 Eighth of January

A folksinger and high school civics teacher named Jimmy Driftwood wrote lyrics to this tune about the War of 1812 for his students and called it "The Battle of New Orleans." Johnny Horton made it famous.

2 Liberty

*This common tune is one of the first that most fiddlers learn.
It sounds especially great with two or three fiddlers playing it in harmony.*

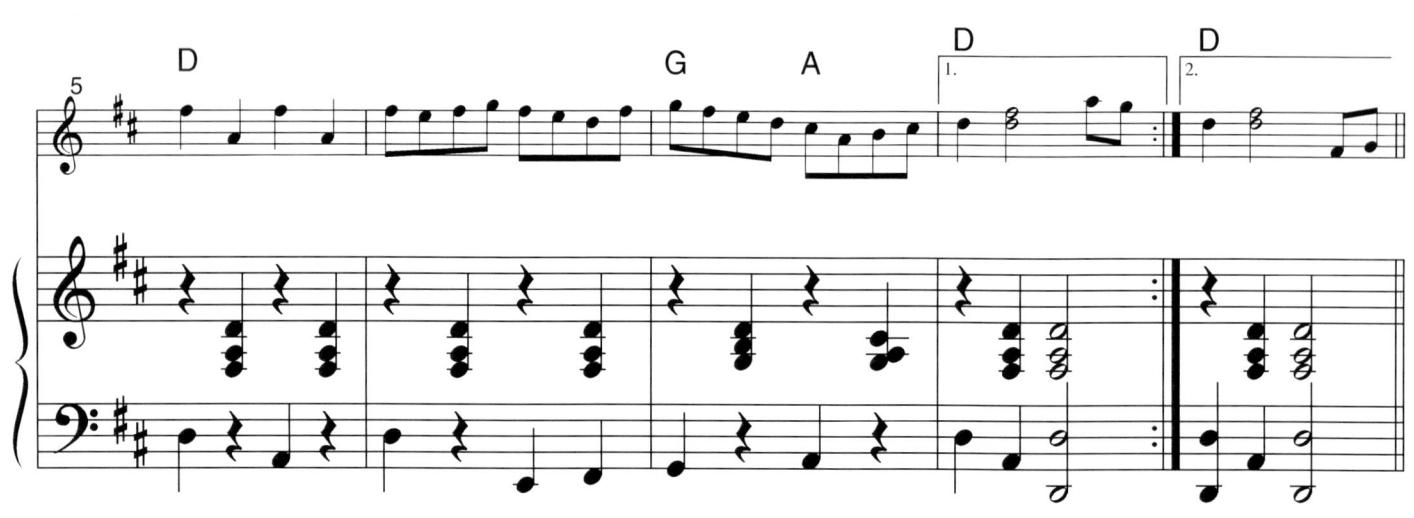

3 St. Anne's Reel

This Canadian tune is popular in jams across North America.

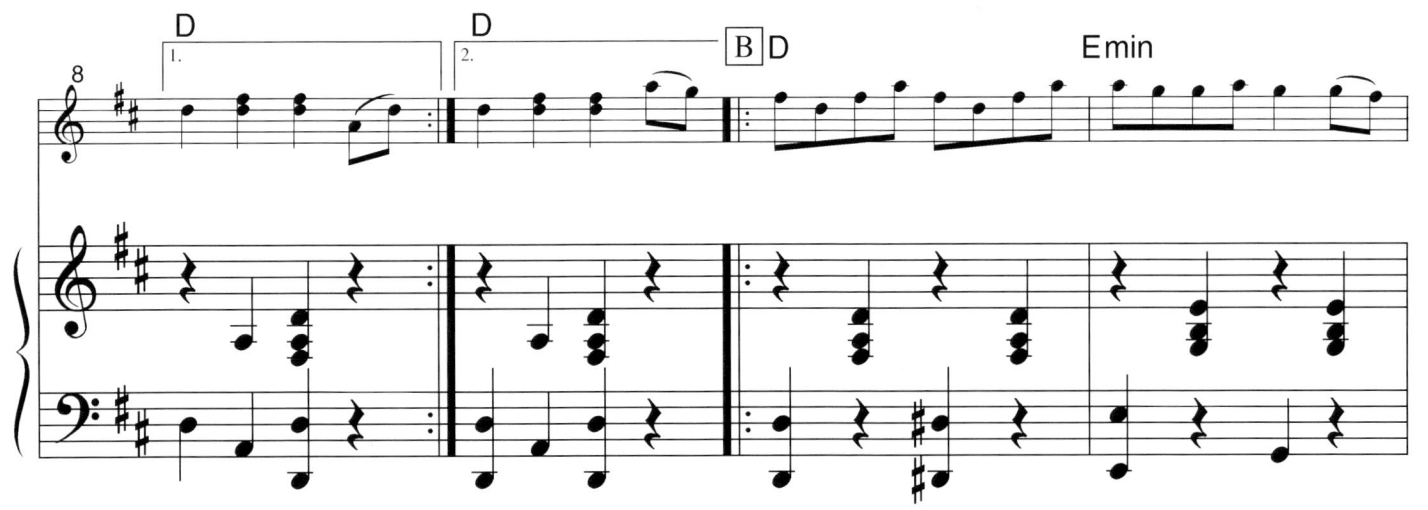

4 Spotted Pony

*This old-time Appalachian tune has always been one of my favorites.
I think the pony is bucking at the beginning of the A section and smoothes out to a gallop at
the beginning of the B section*

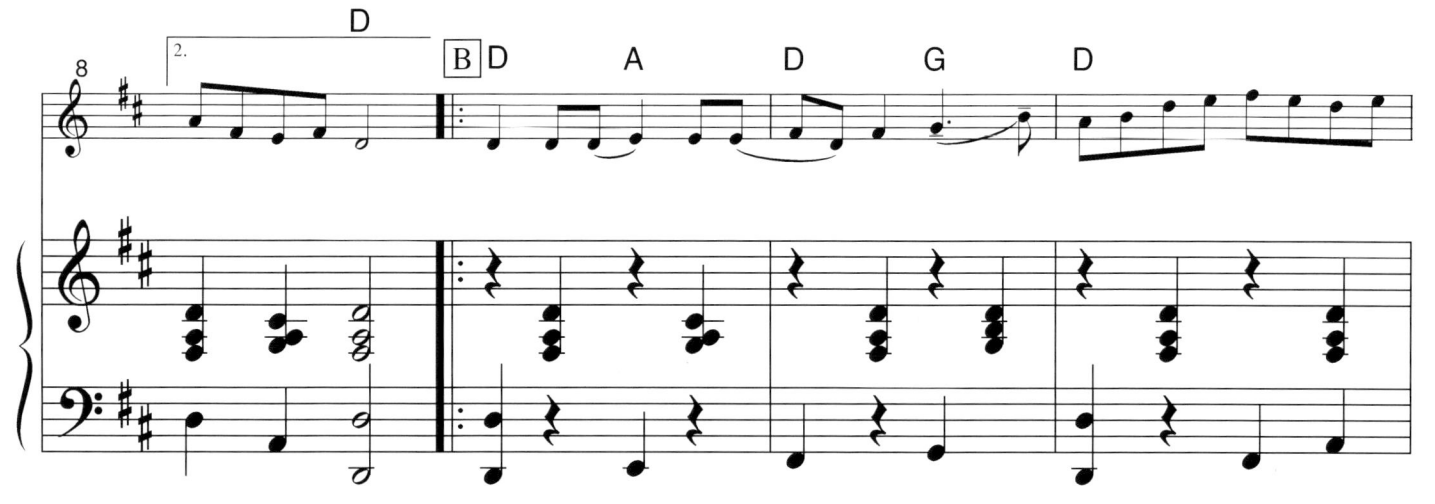

5 Cuckoo's Nest

This is a popular reel from the Canadian and New England fiddle tradition.

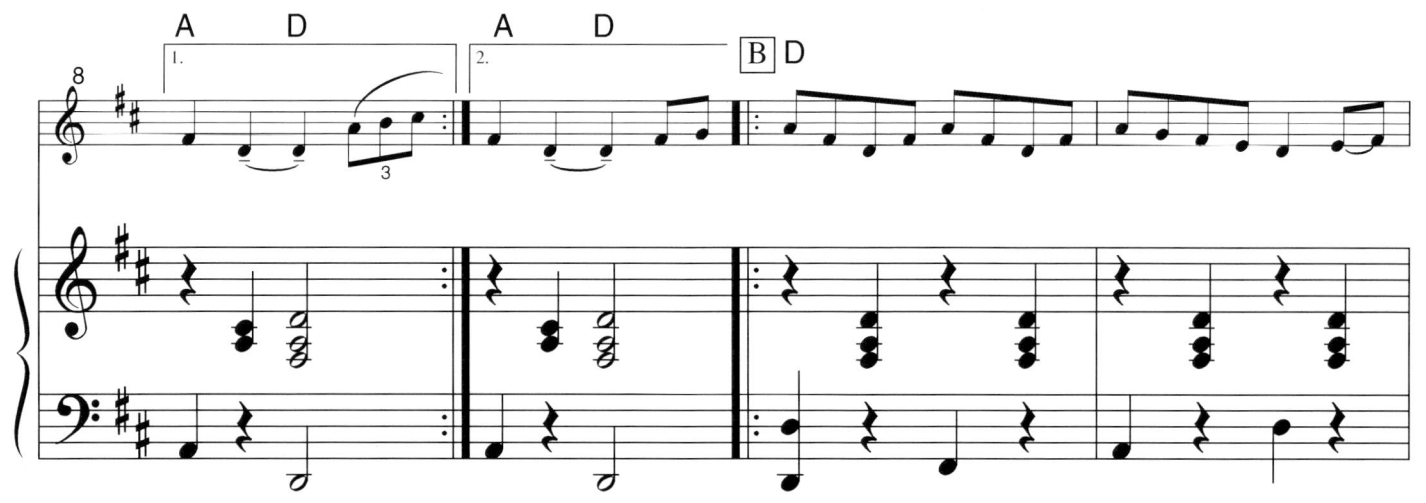

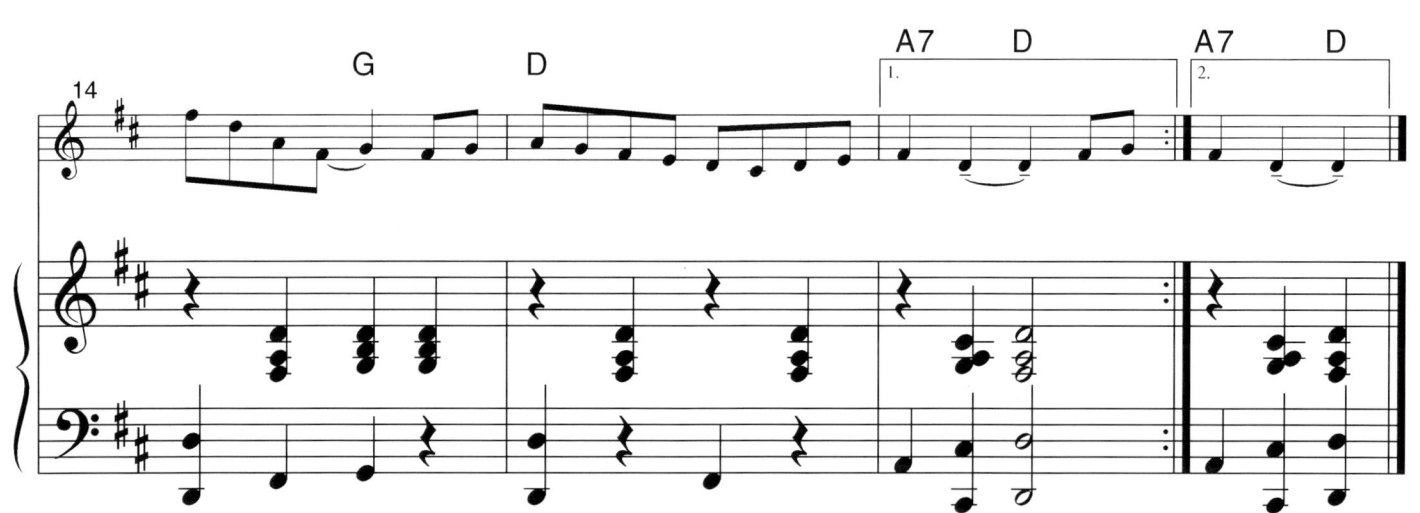

6 Old Joe Clark

This tune was written before 1840 and is thought to be named after an African-American man from Kentucky. This version is more advanced than the one in Volume 1.

7 Soldier's Joy

*"Soldier's Joy" was what English soldiers called their payday.
Fiddlers from all over Europe and North America play this tune.*

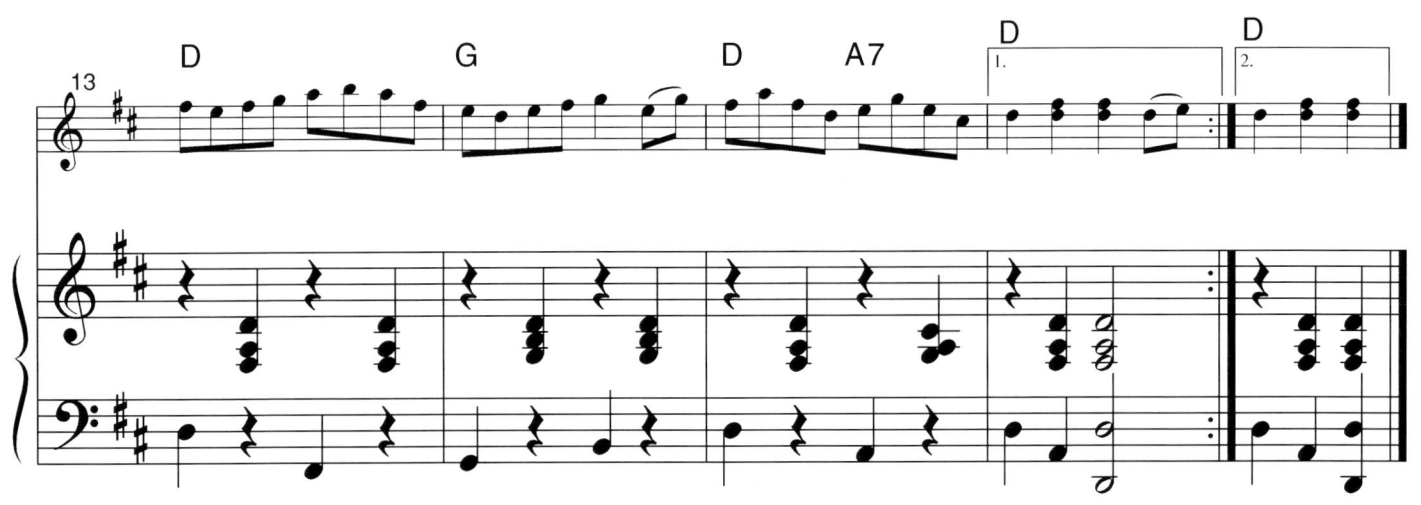

8 Swallowtail Jig

This is a popular Irish jig (6/8 time). The first and fourth beats of each measure are accented.

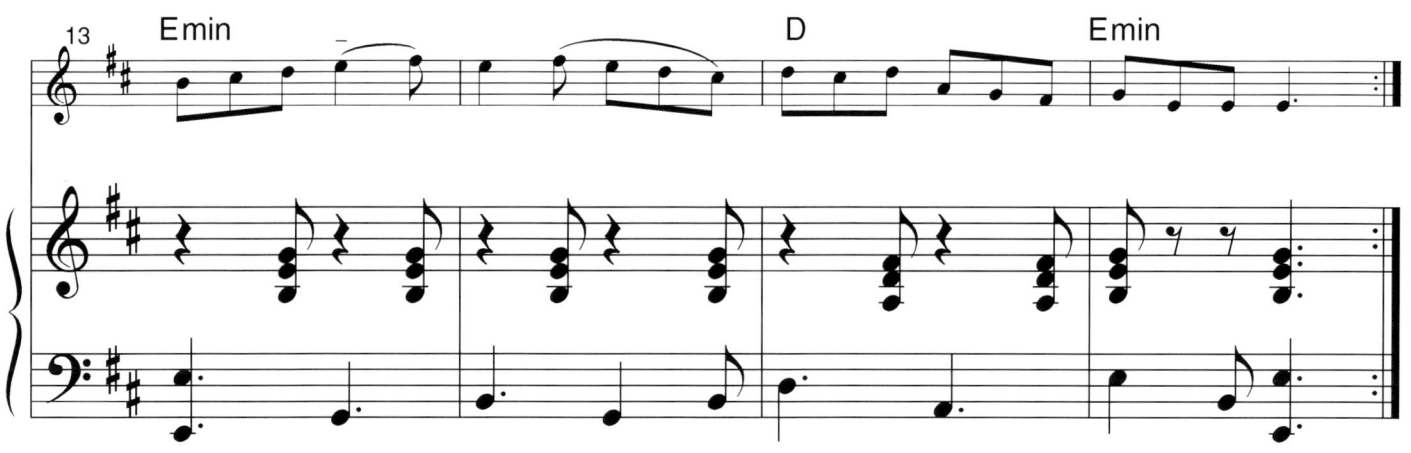

9 June Apple

This Appalachian old-time tune is played throughout the United States.

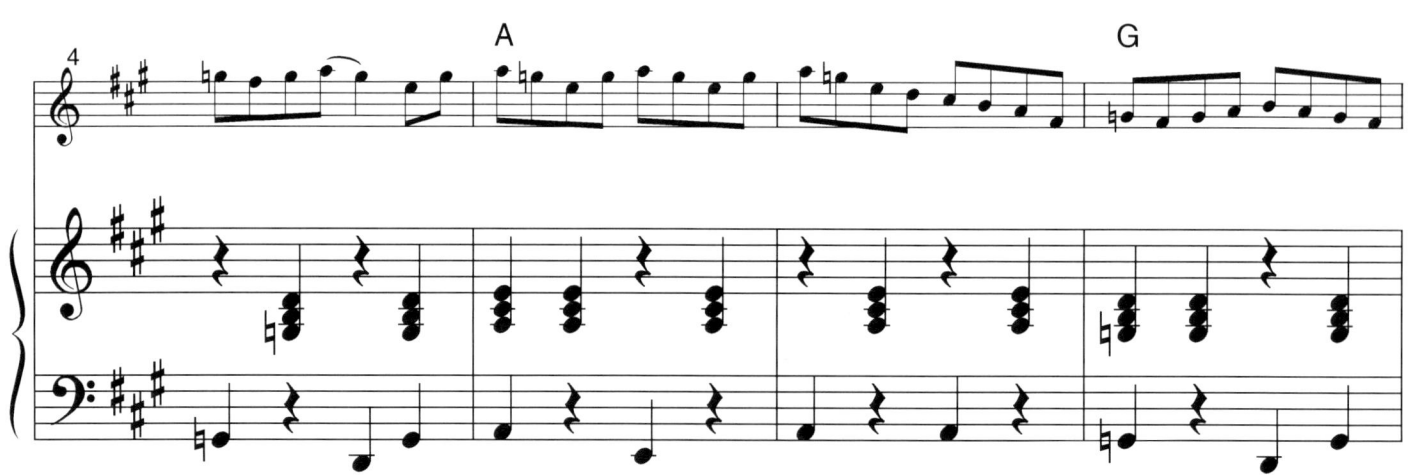

10 Fisher's Hornpipe

Although this tune was originally played as a hornpipe (with a dotted rhythm), American fiddlers usually "straighten out" the eighth notes, as in a reel. This was probably originally done to accompany American dancing (e.g., squares, contras, and clogging), which is much better suited to straight rather than dotted rhythms. The third part is optional.

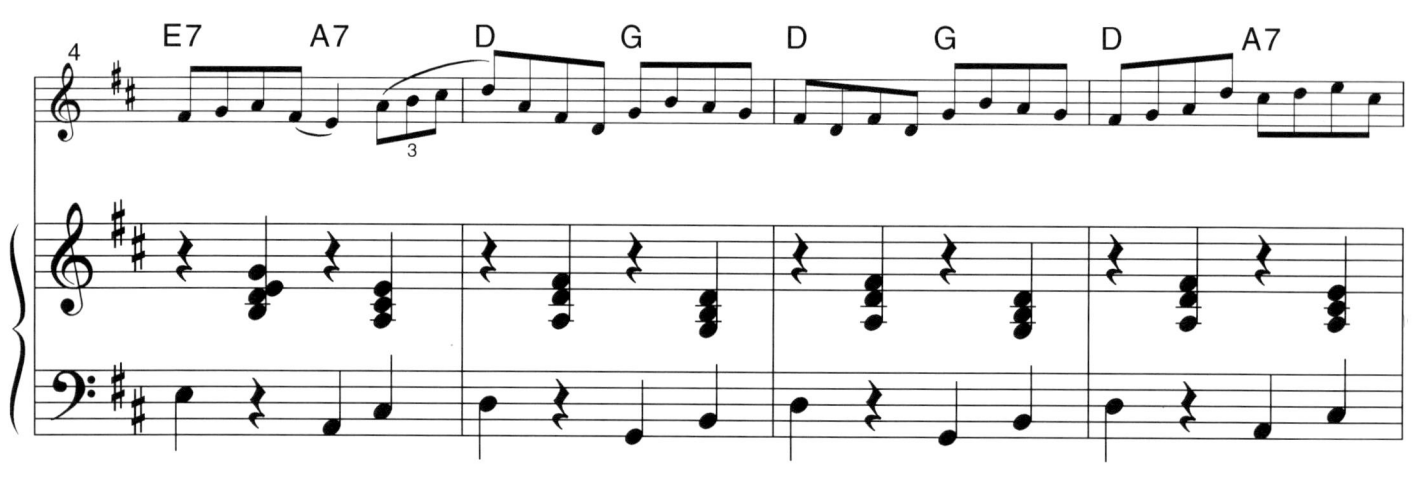

11 Liza Jane

You may recognize the similarities between this tune and "Cairo" from Volume 1, although the A and B parts are reversed.

12 Arkansas Traveler

*This old vaudeville tune has had countless humorous lyrics written to its melody.
I first heard this as "I had a little baby bumblebee, won't my momma be so proud of me..."*

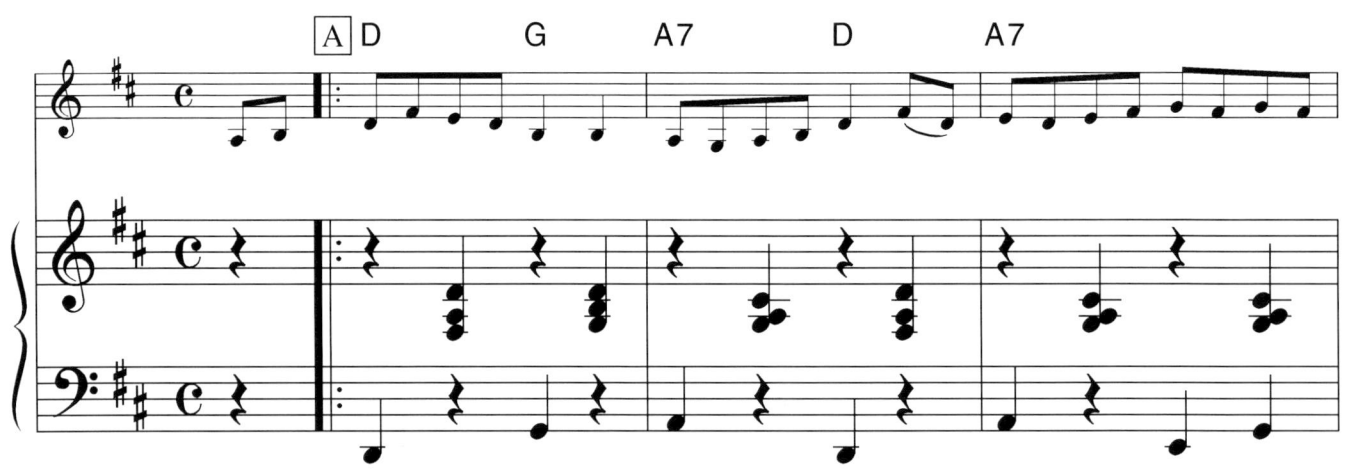

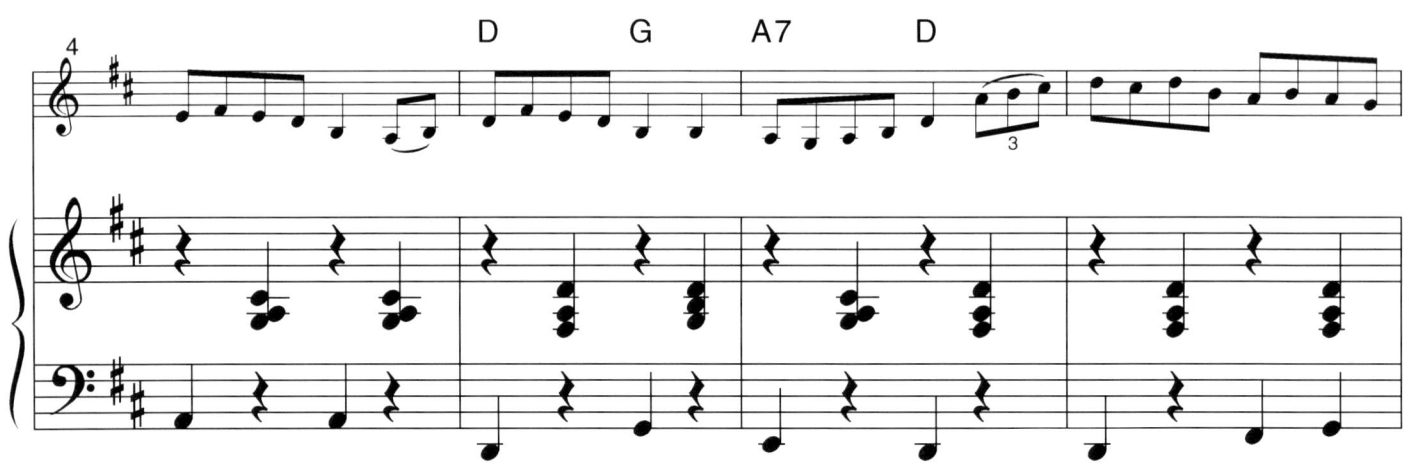

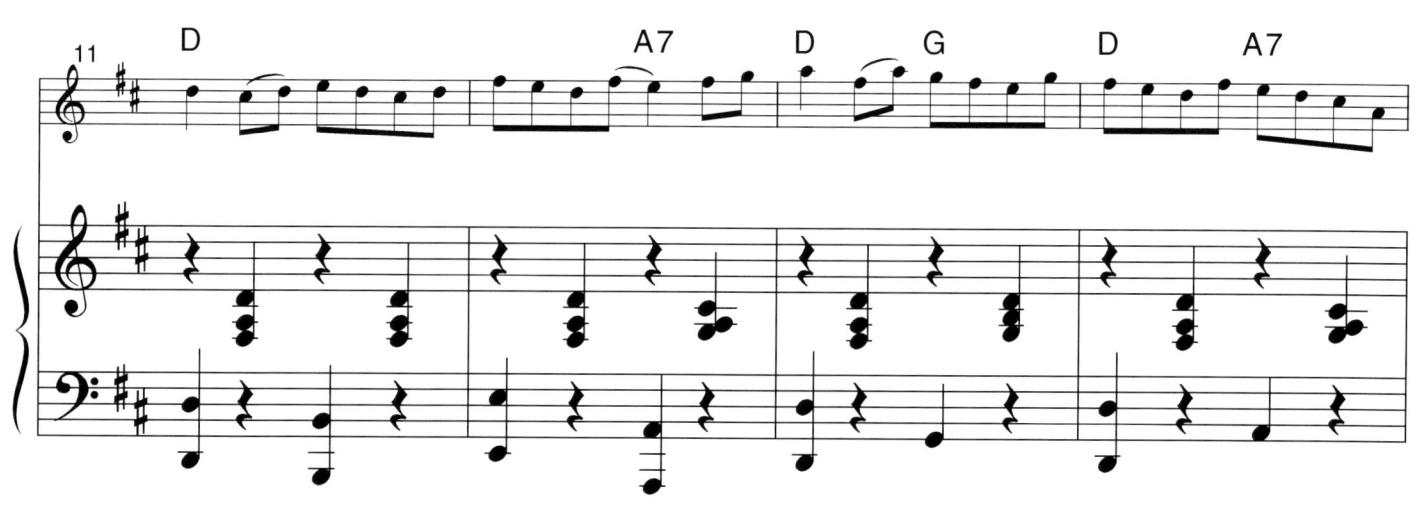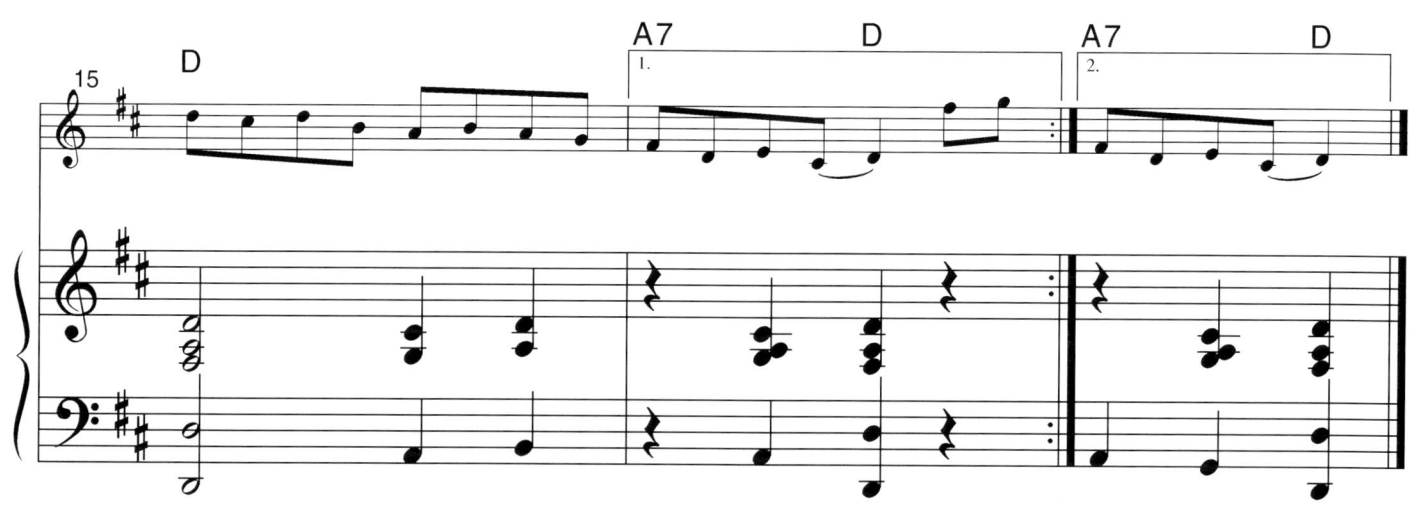

13 Devil's Dream

Some religious groups in the South considered dancing to be a sin. The fiddle got the nickname "The Devil's Box" because it made people want to dance.

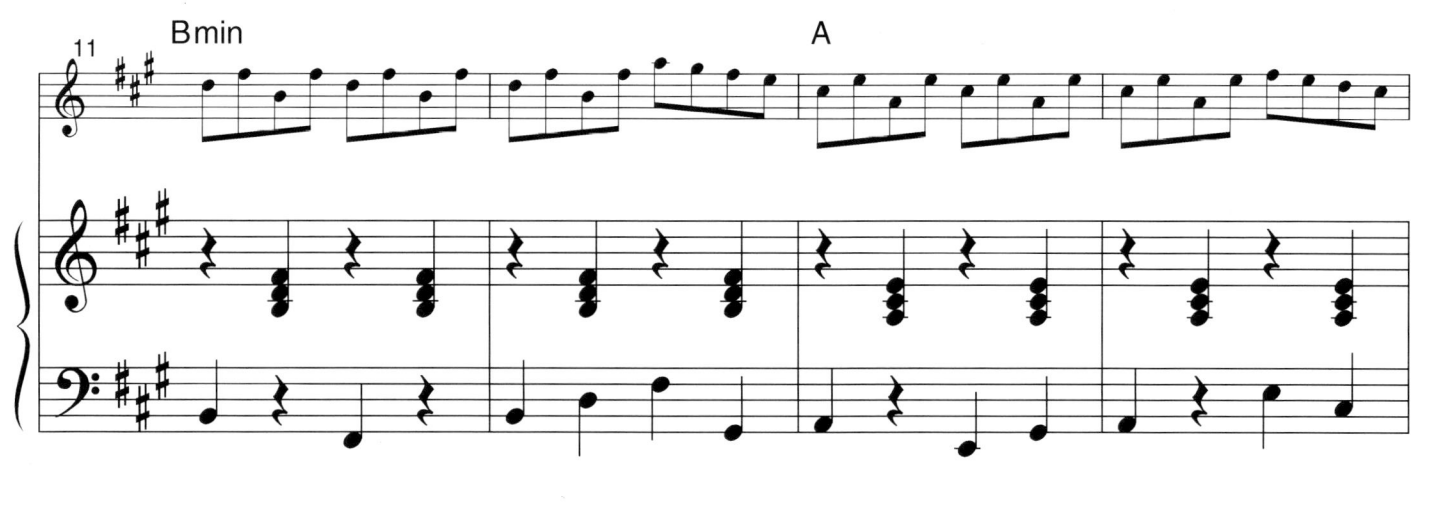

14 Westphalia Waltz

German immigrants probably brought this beautiful waltz to America. It is a very popular choice at fiddle contests throughout the country.

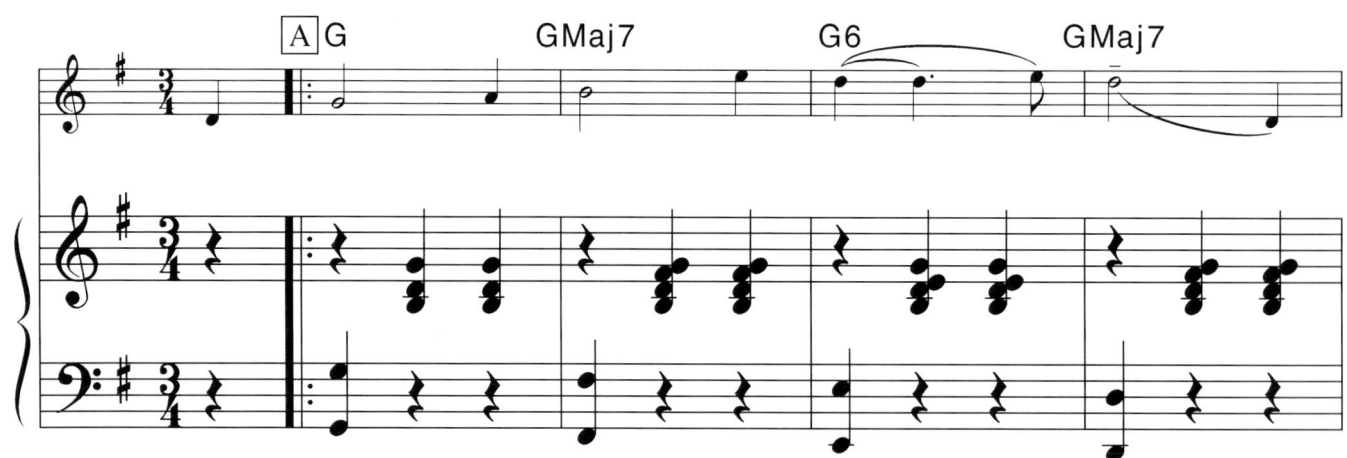

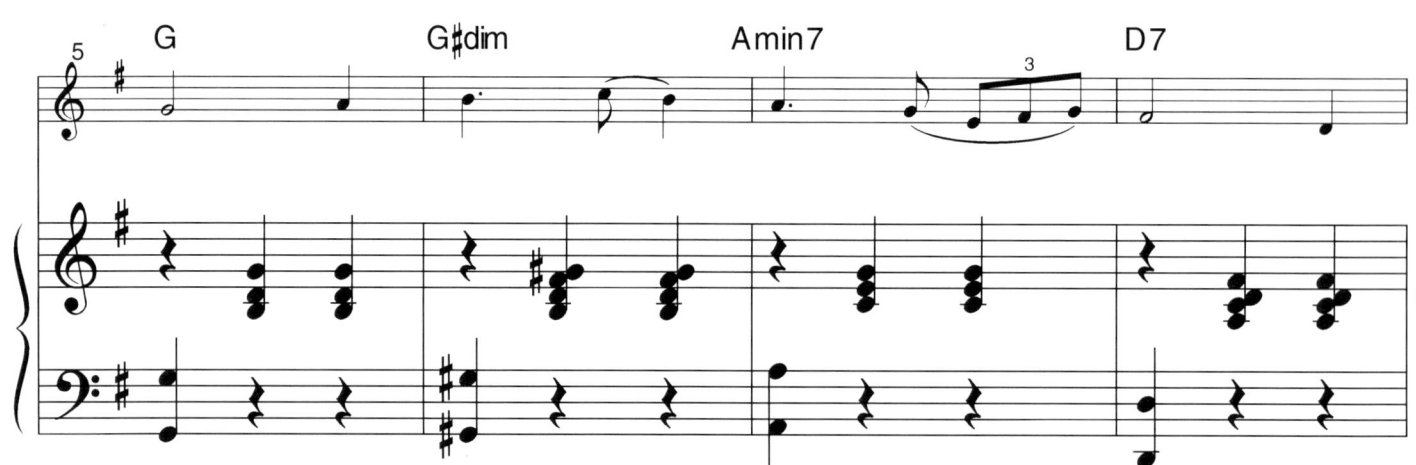

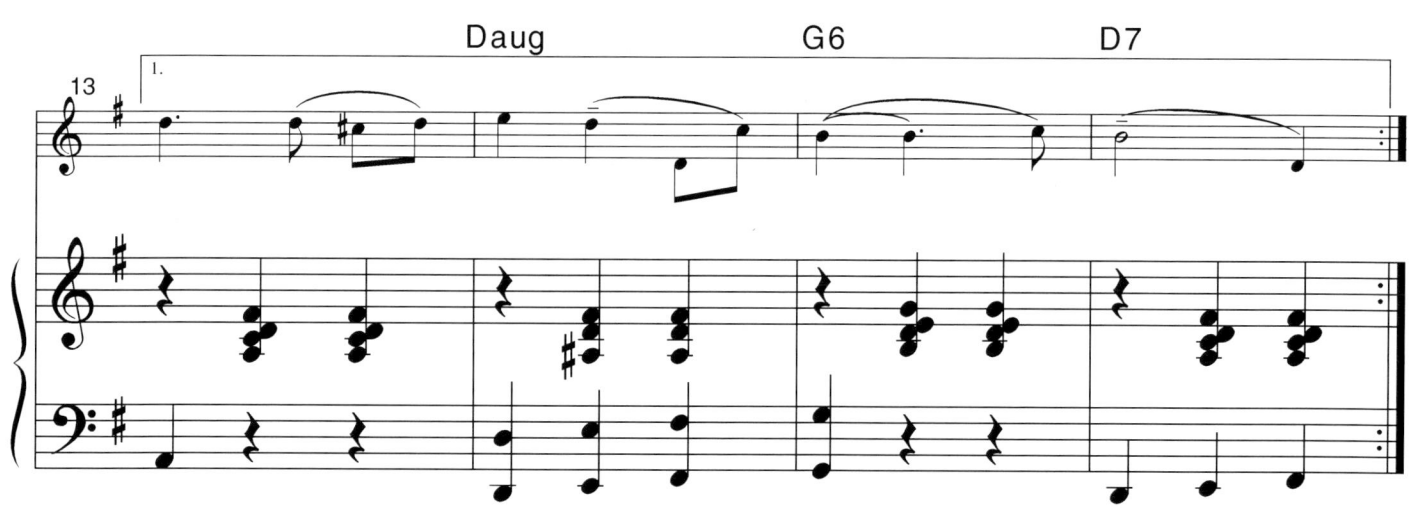
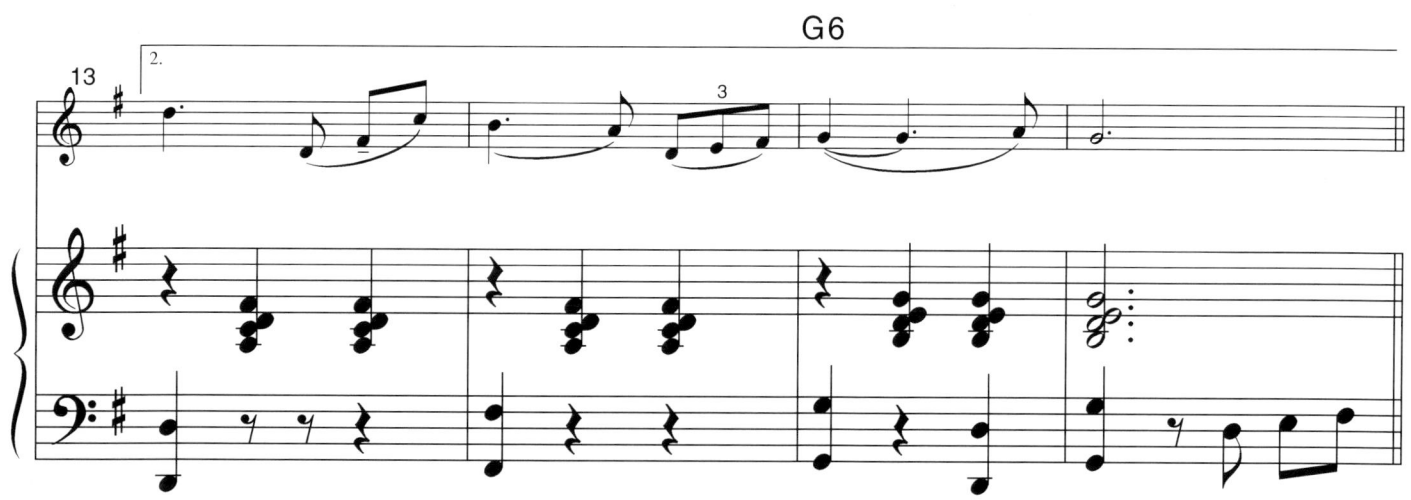

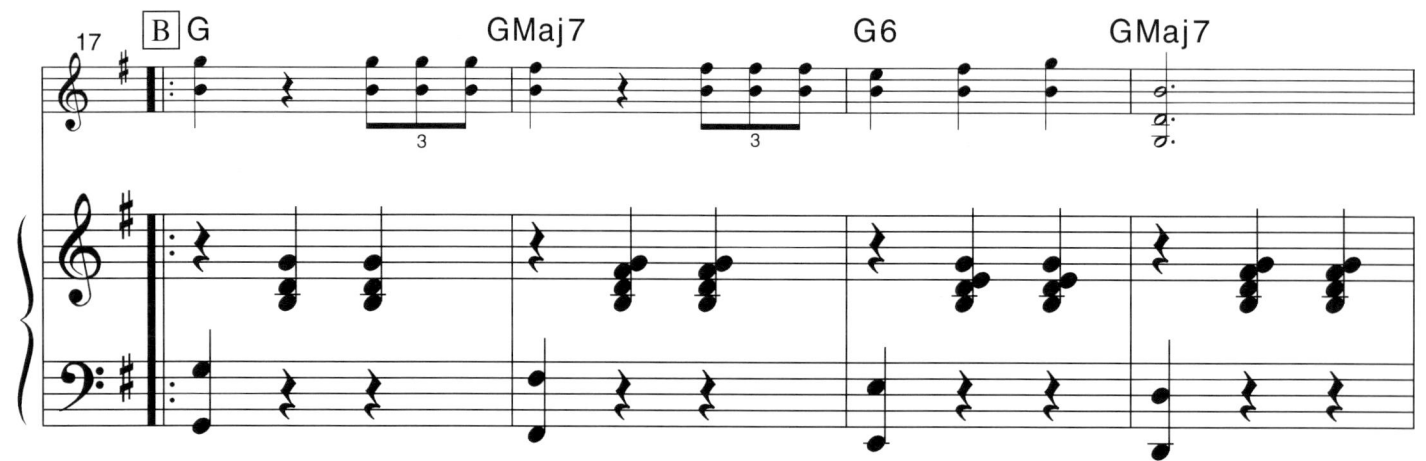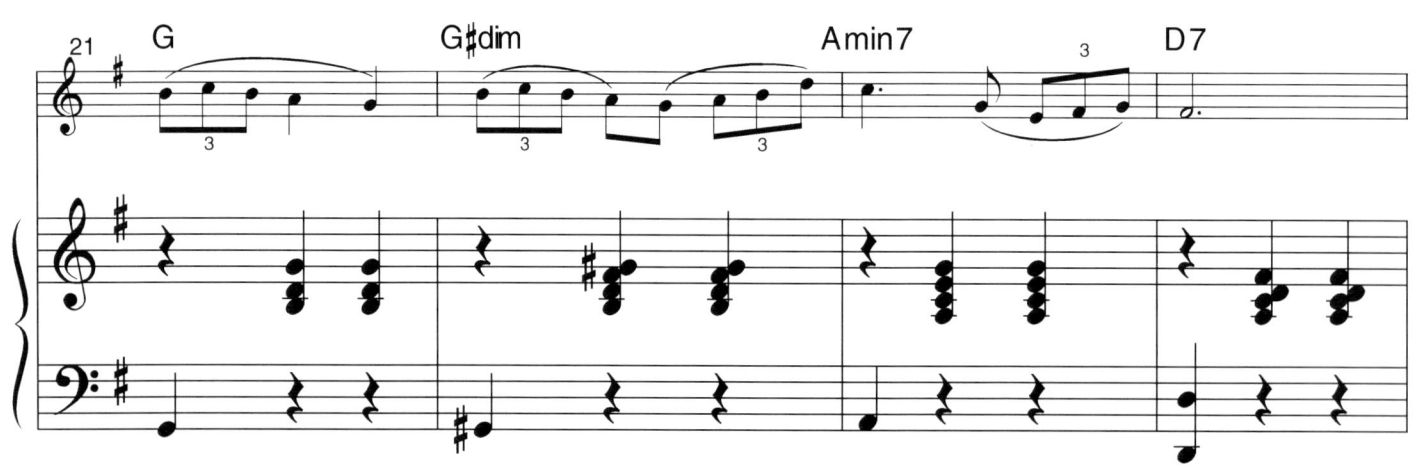

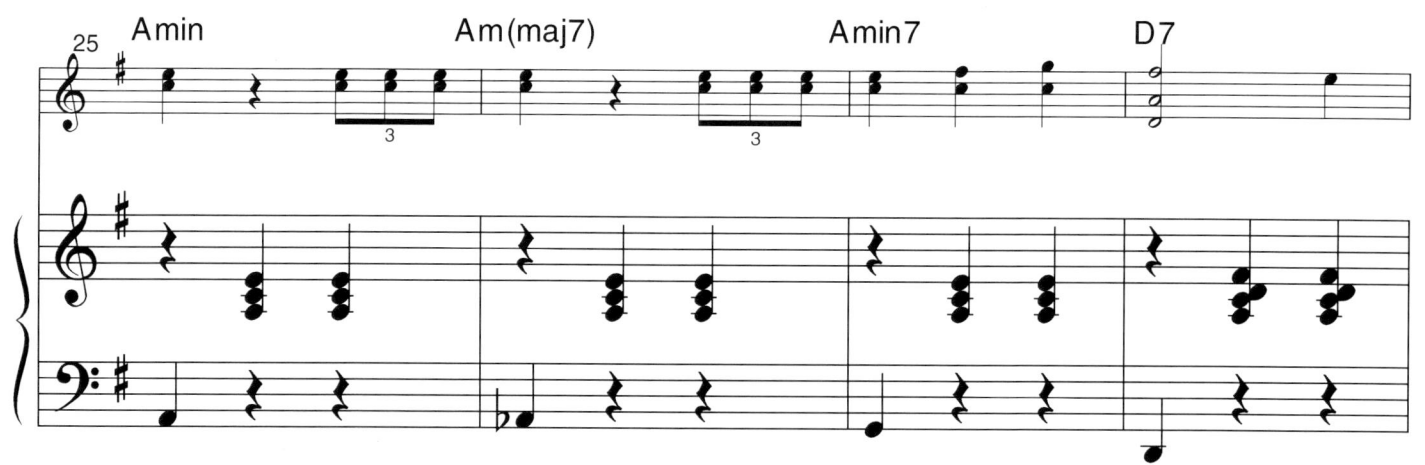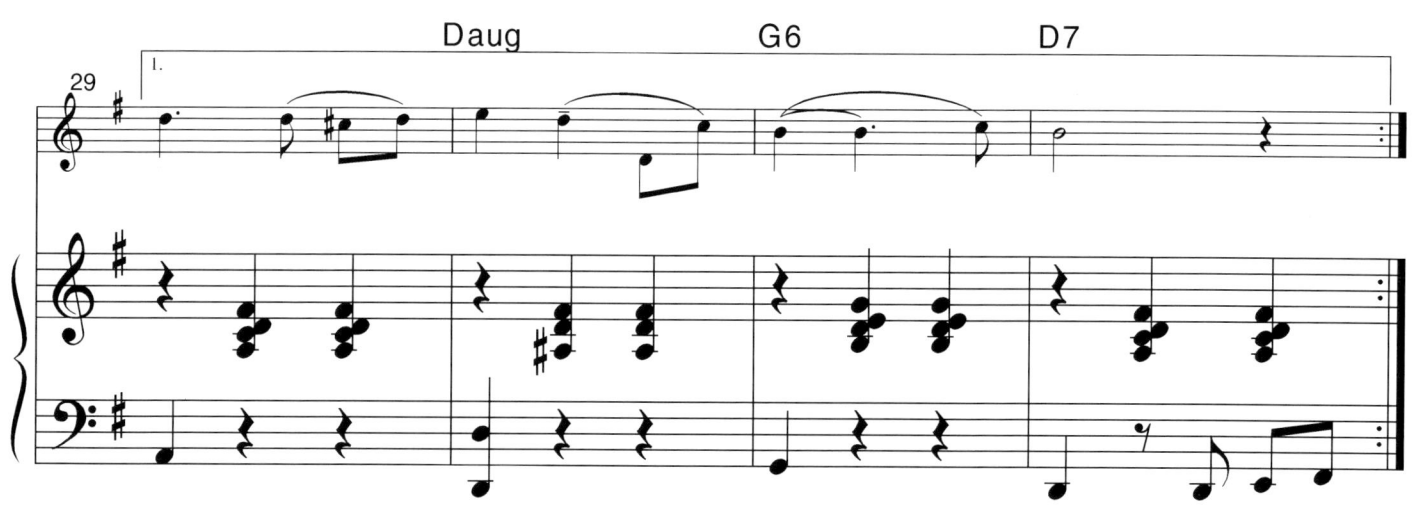

15 Ragtime Annie

This tune is an old ragtime piece that fiddlers have taken as their own.

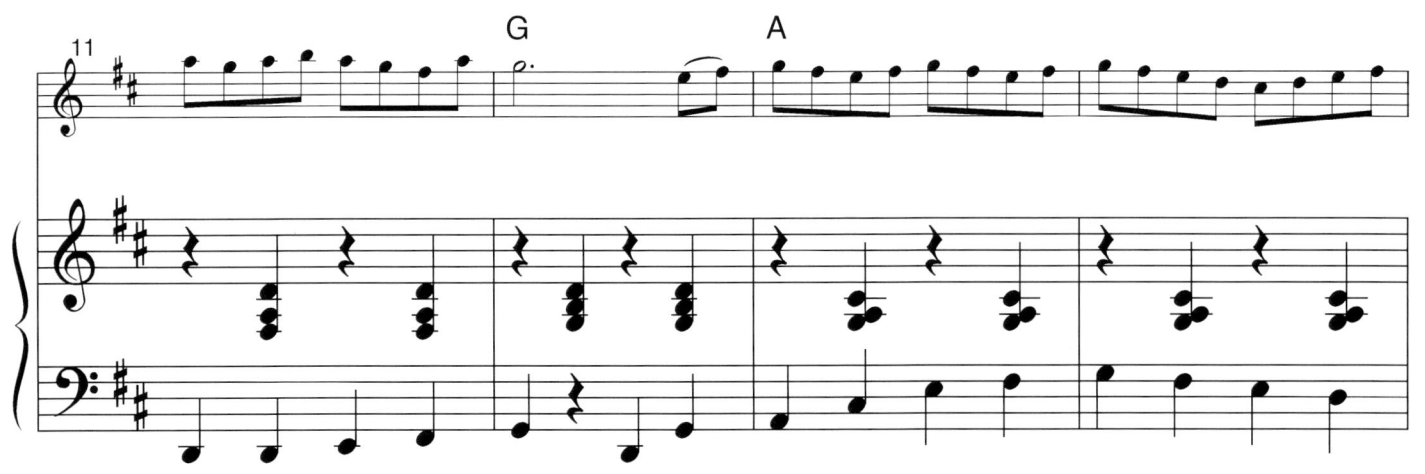

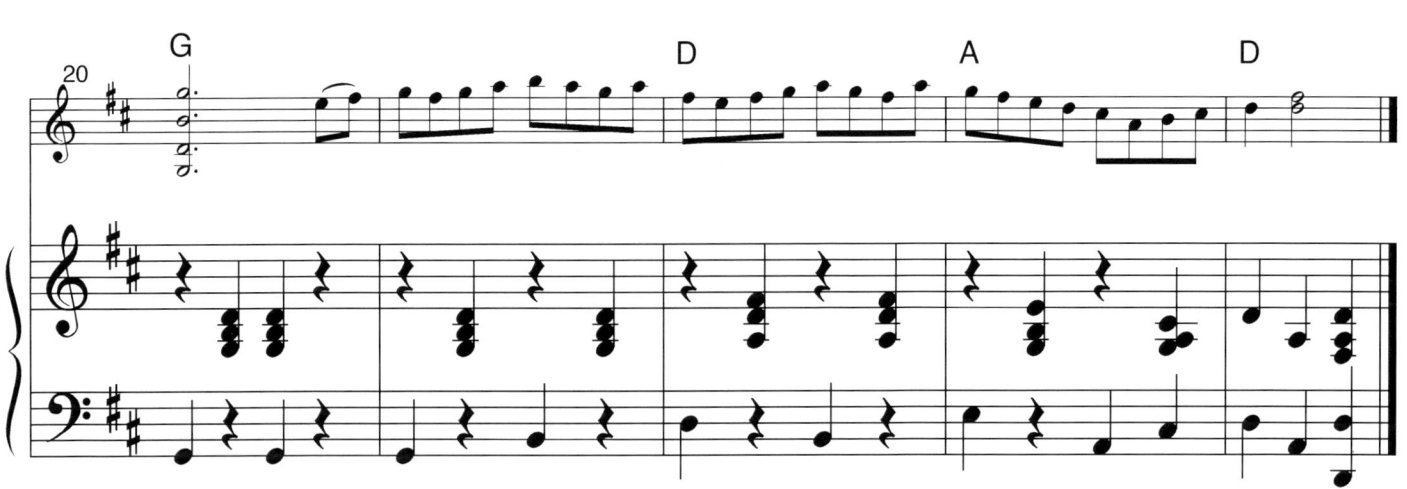

16 Golden Anniversary Waltz

*A golden anniversary is celebrated at a couple's 50th year of marriage.
It's a significant event, certainly worthy of a beautiful waltz.*

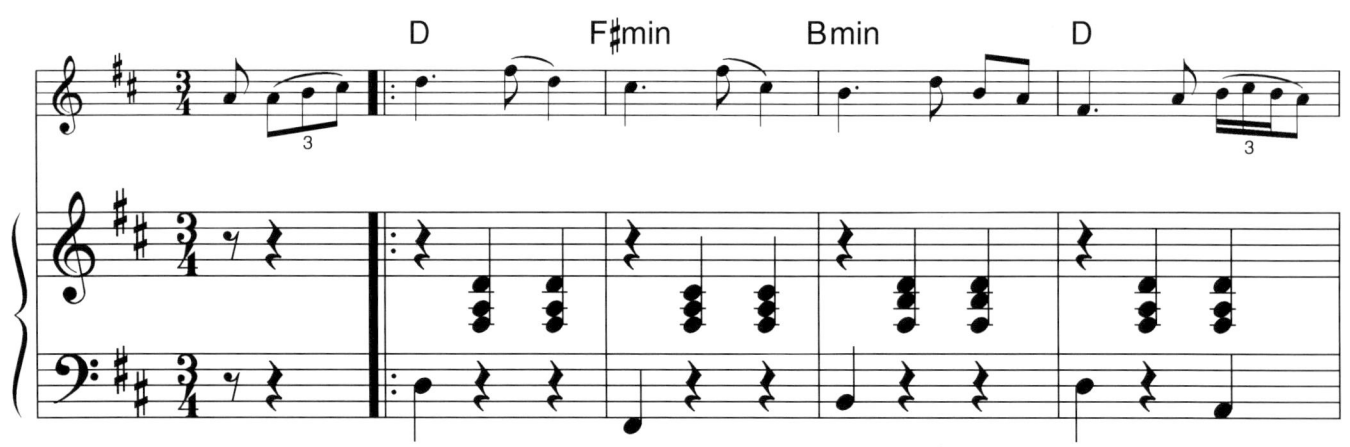

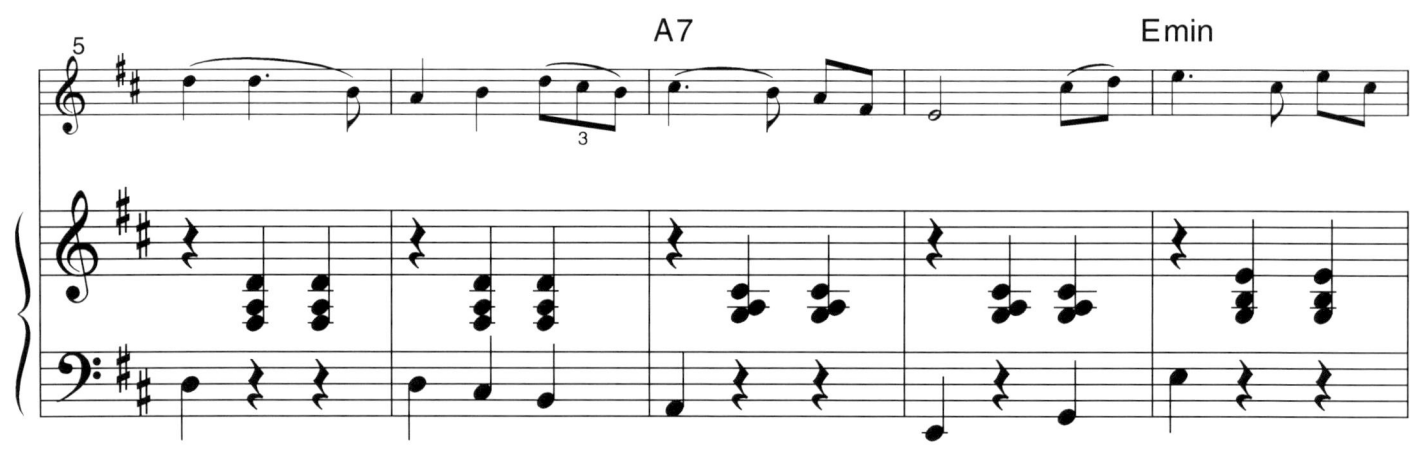

17 Big John McNeil

When this classic Canadian tune is played with a driving band, there is hardly anything finer.

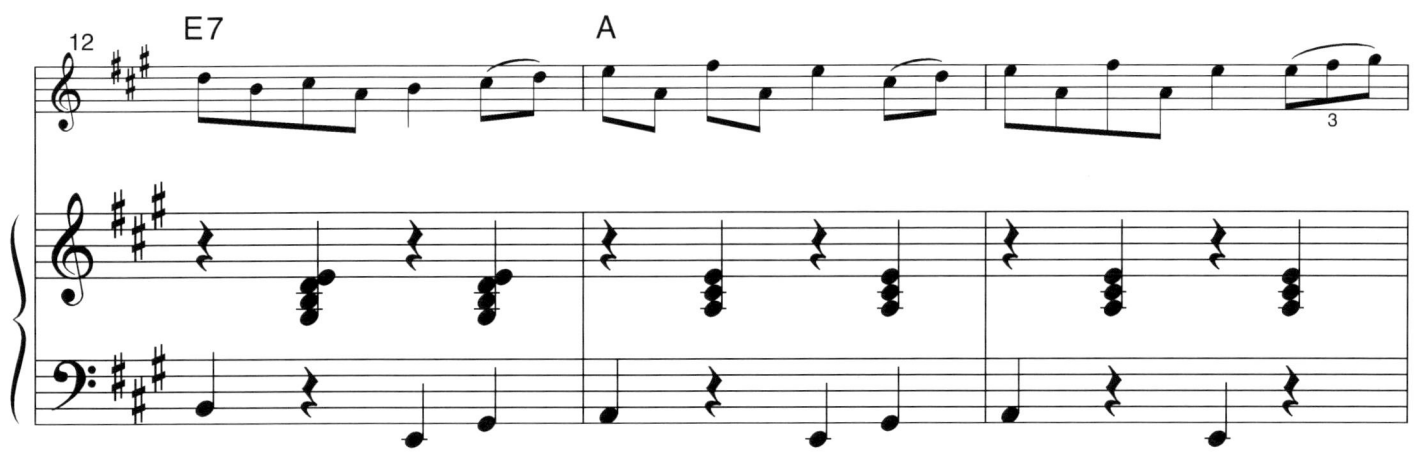
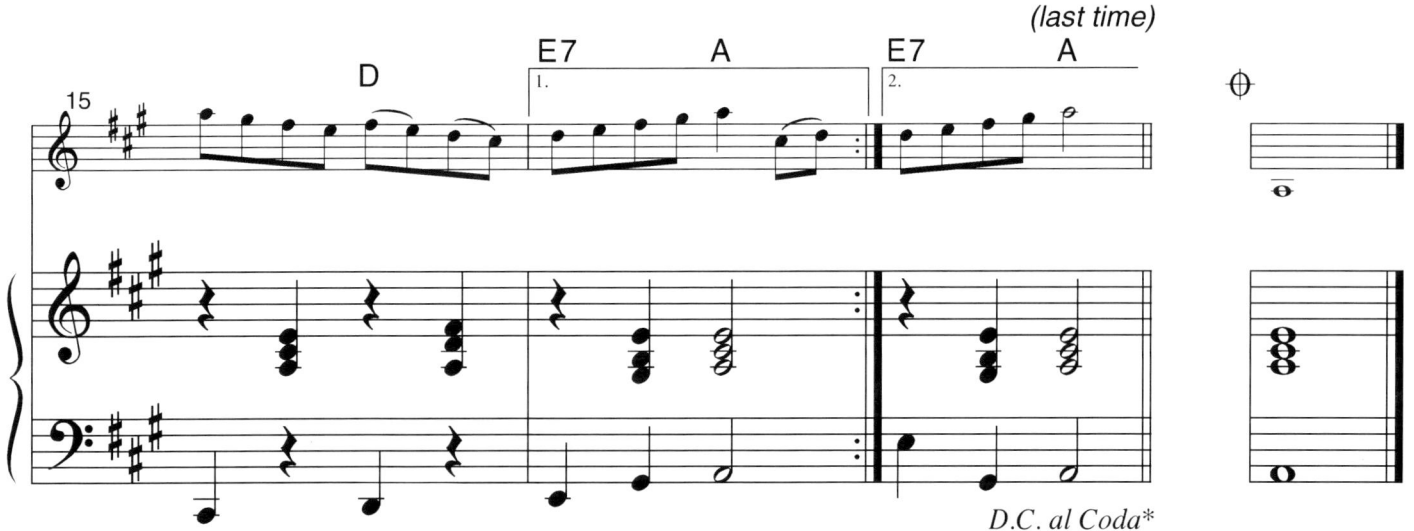

*D.C. al Coda**

* Repeat form as desired. Take coda last time

18 Star of the County Down

This is a beautiful Irish waltz.

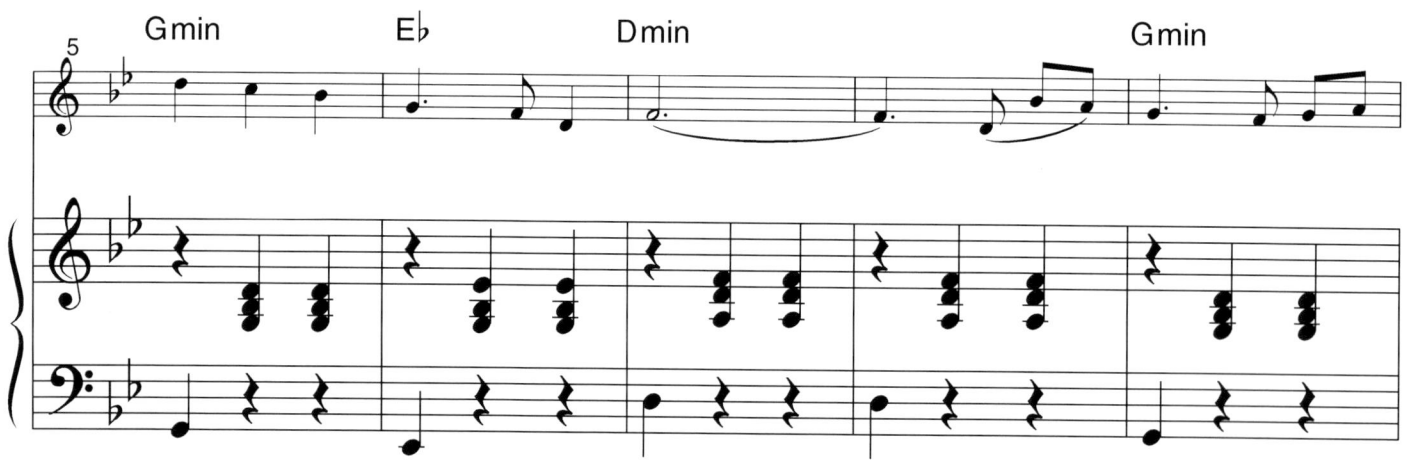

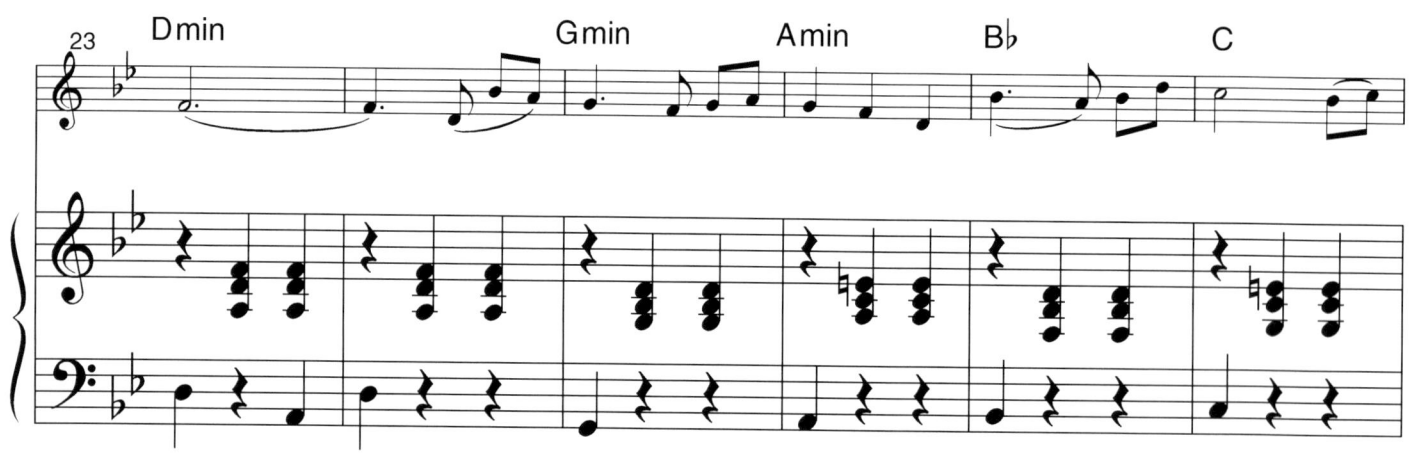

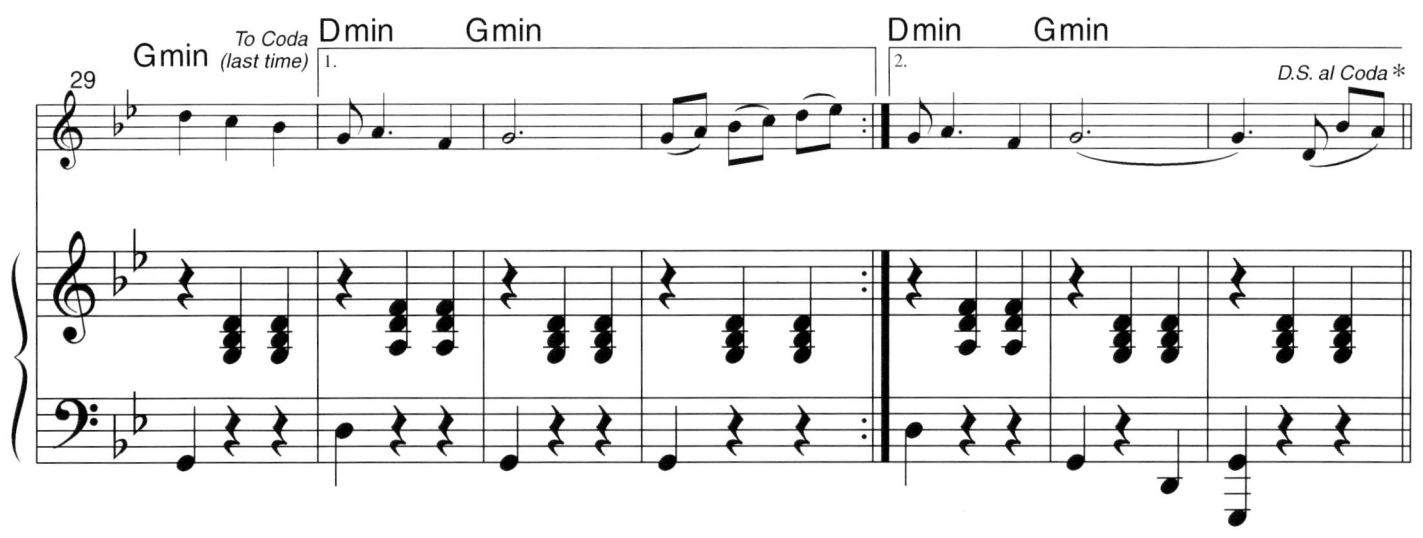

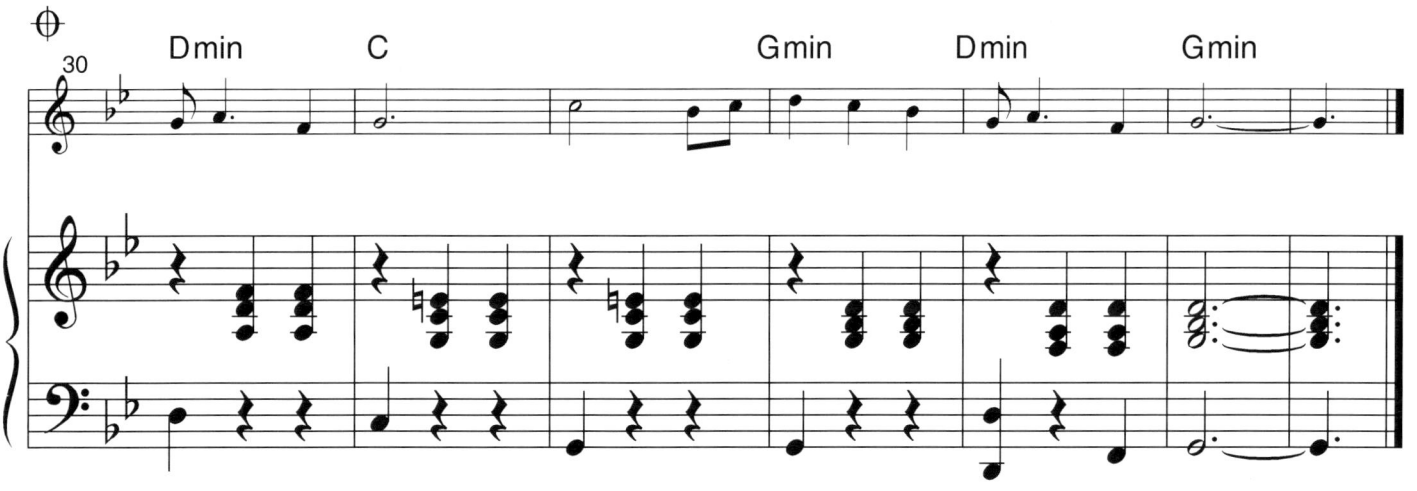

* Repeat A and B as desired.
Last time through B, take
coda instead of 2nd ending.

43

19 Benny's Favorite

©1999 Brian Wicklund BMI
This tune has become legendary in the Teton Valley of Idaho.

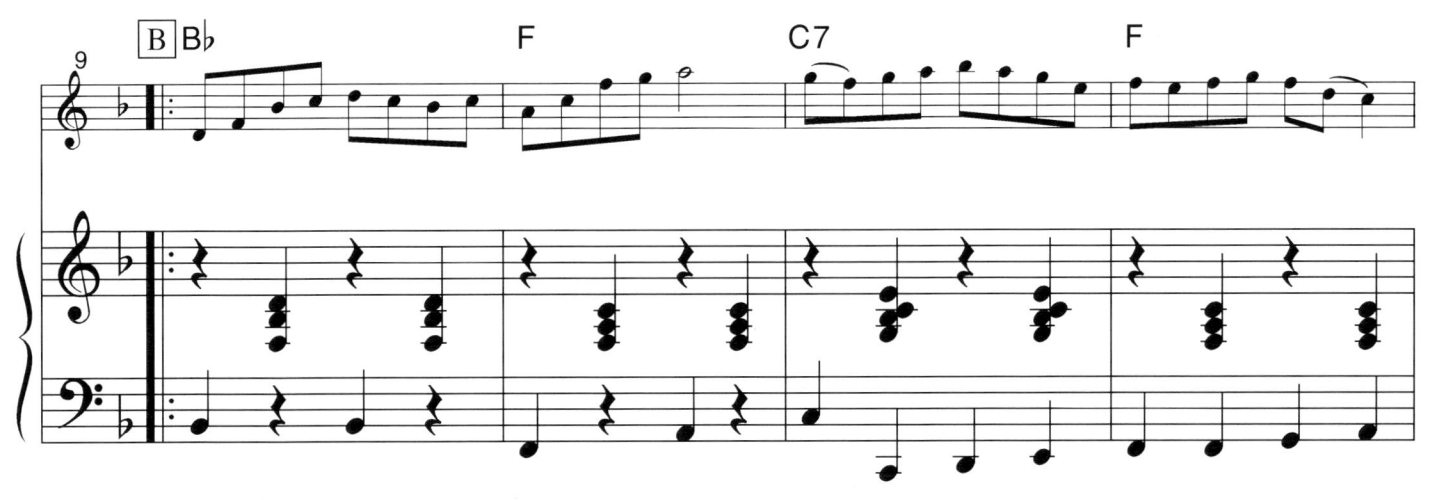
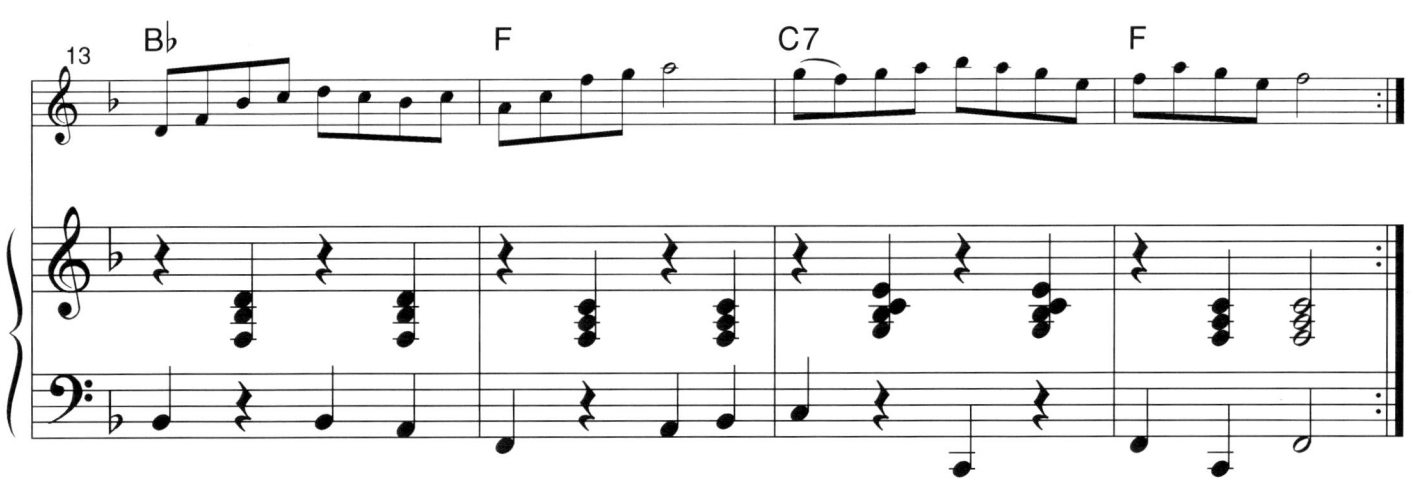

Marie Clare

This is a jaunty French-Canadian tune in B♭.

Bernard the Butterfly

©1988 Brian Wicklund, Witches Tree Publishing, BMI
*The image that came to mind as I was writing this tune was of a very large,
friendly, but extremely dumb butterfly.*

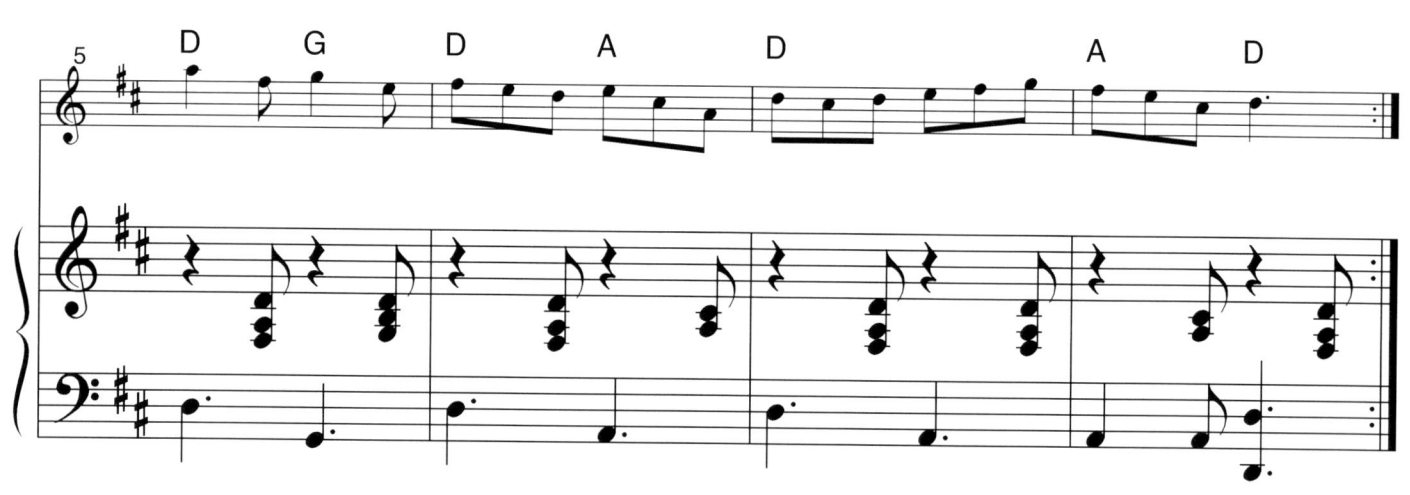

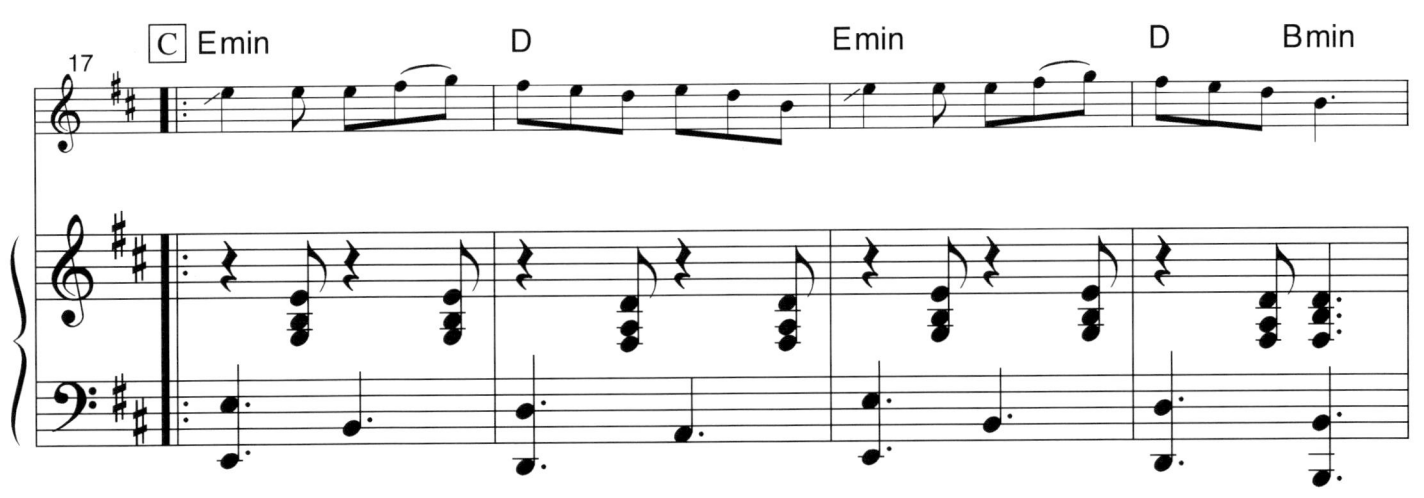
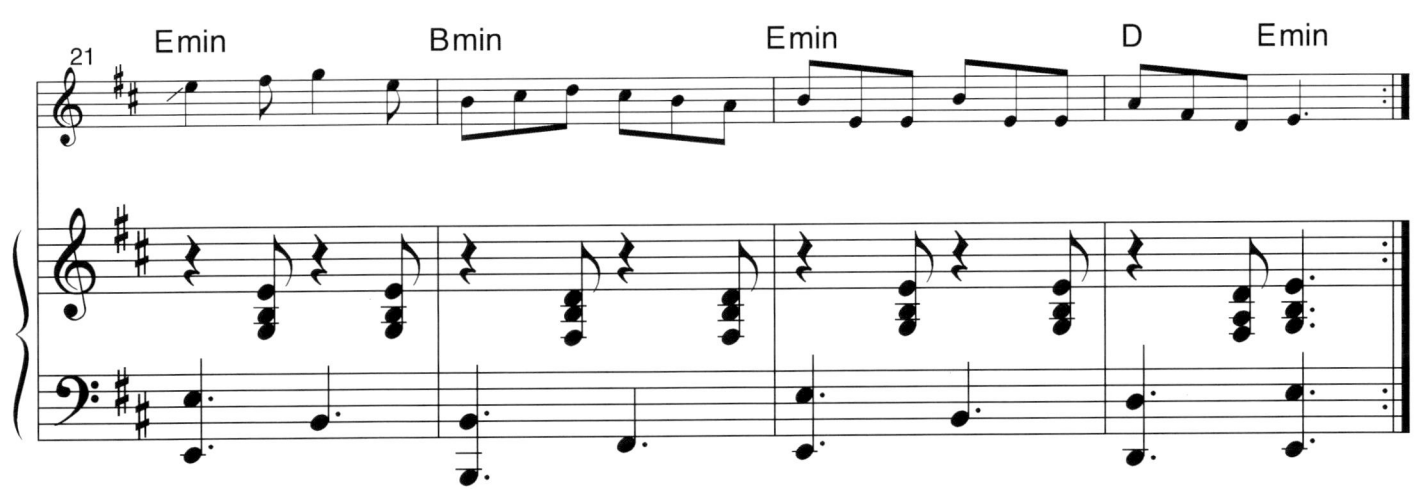

22 Flop-Eared Mule

This hoedown changes from the key of D in A to the key of A in B.
I suggest ending this tune in the key in which it begins,
so finish the tune with one A and an ending tag in the key of D.

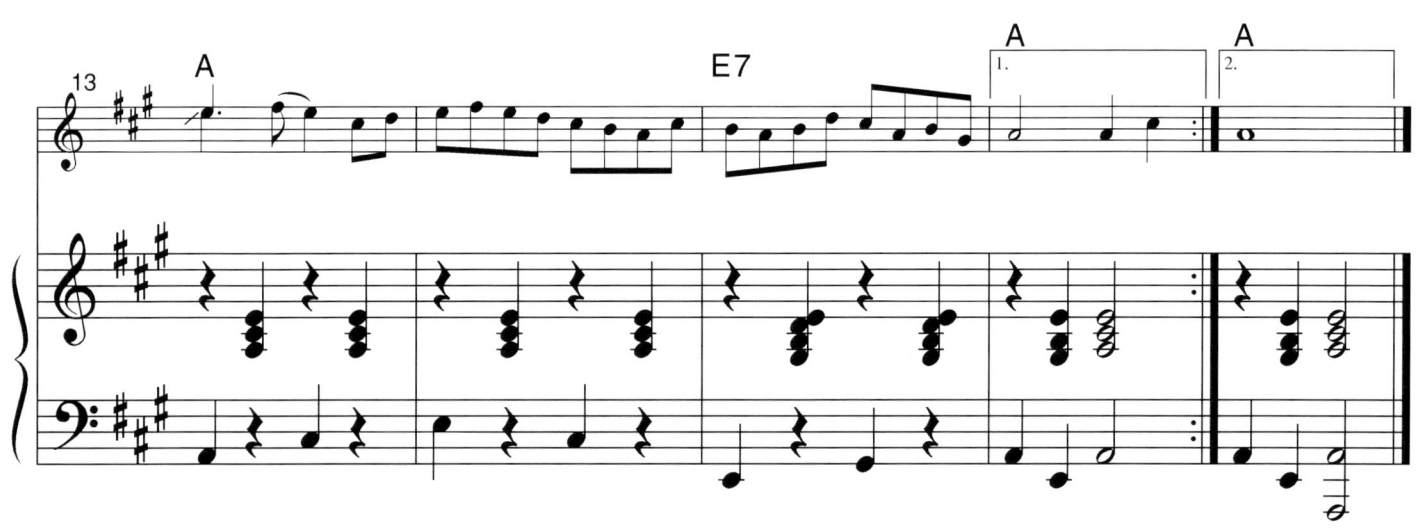

23 Swampwalk

©1988 Brian Wicklund, Witches Tree Publishing, BMI
Lake Beulah in Wisconsin is the site of a folk music camp and a huge marsh.
This tune came to me after a moonlit stroll along the swamp's boardwalk.

52

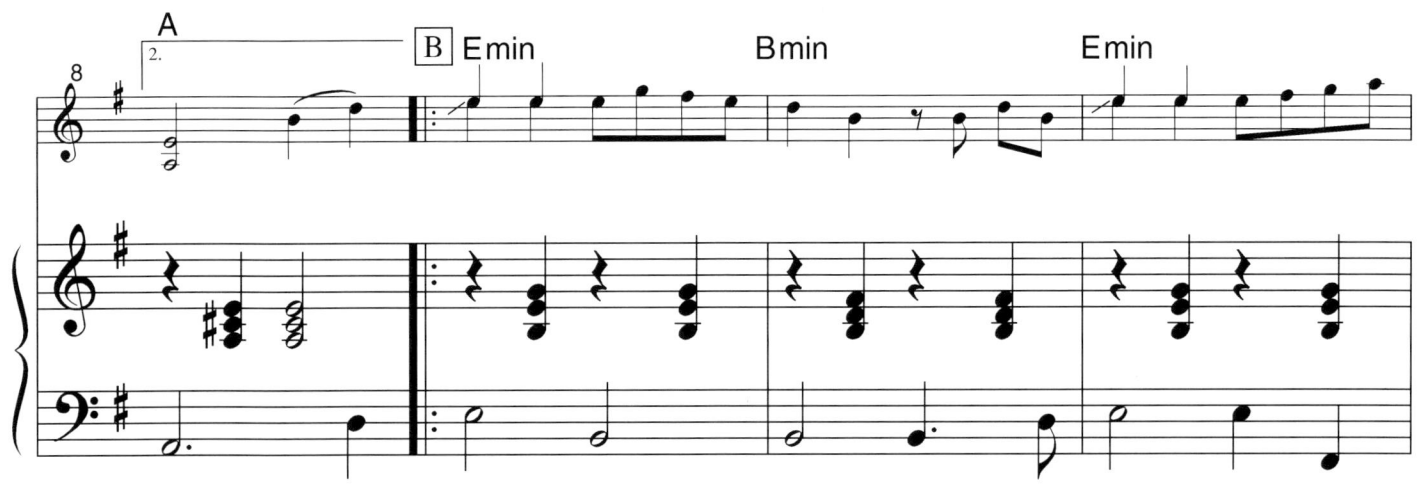

24 Don't Come Home, Johnny

One can only guess at the naming of this driving Appalachian tune. I learned it from Tim O'Brien.

54

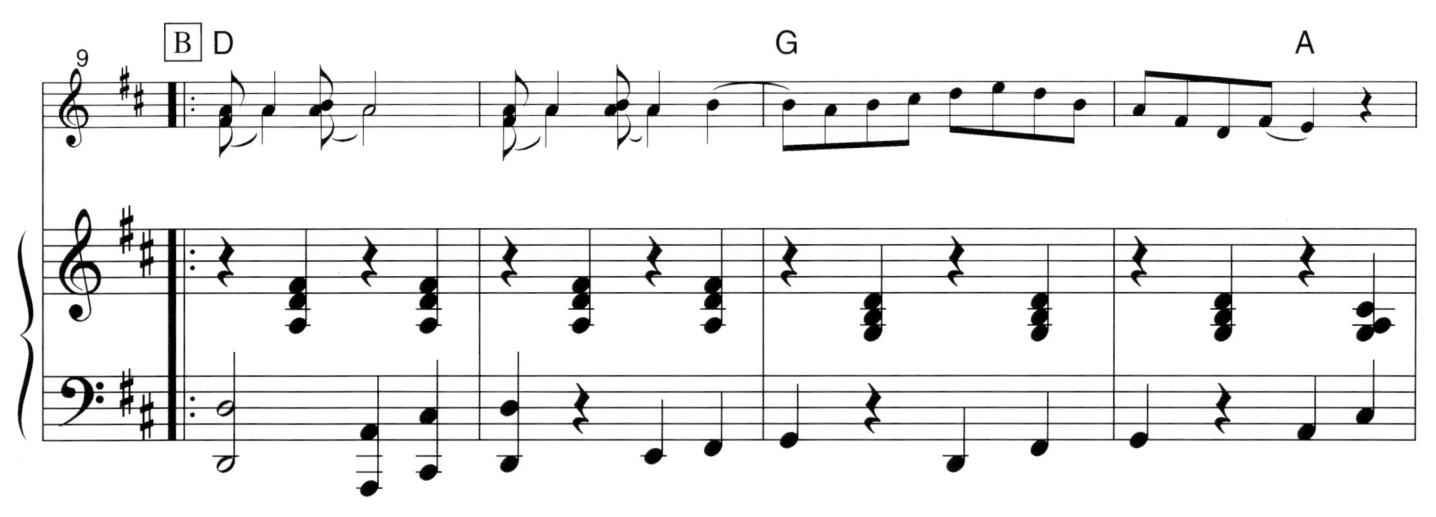

25 Forked Deer

Also called "Forky Deer," this tune has found its way into many fiddle styles, such as old-time, bluegrass, and Texas. A forked deer is one that has begun to grow antlers.

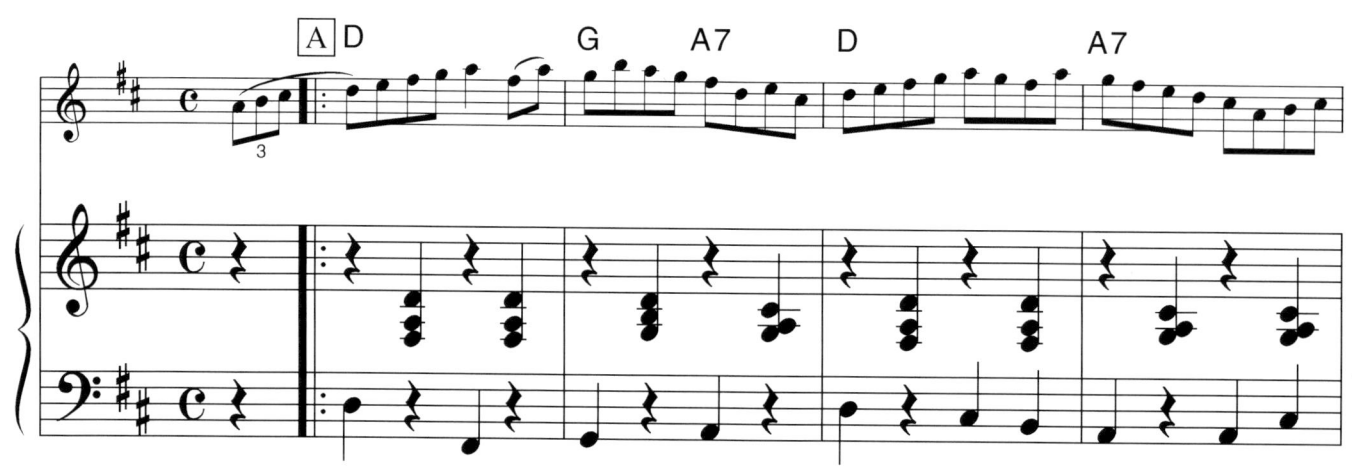

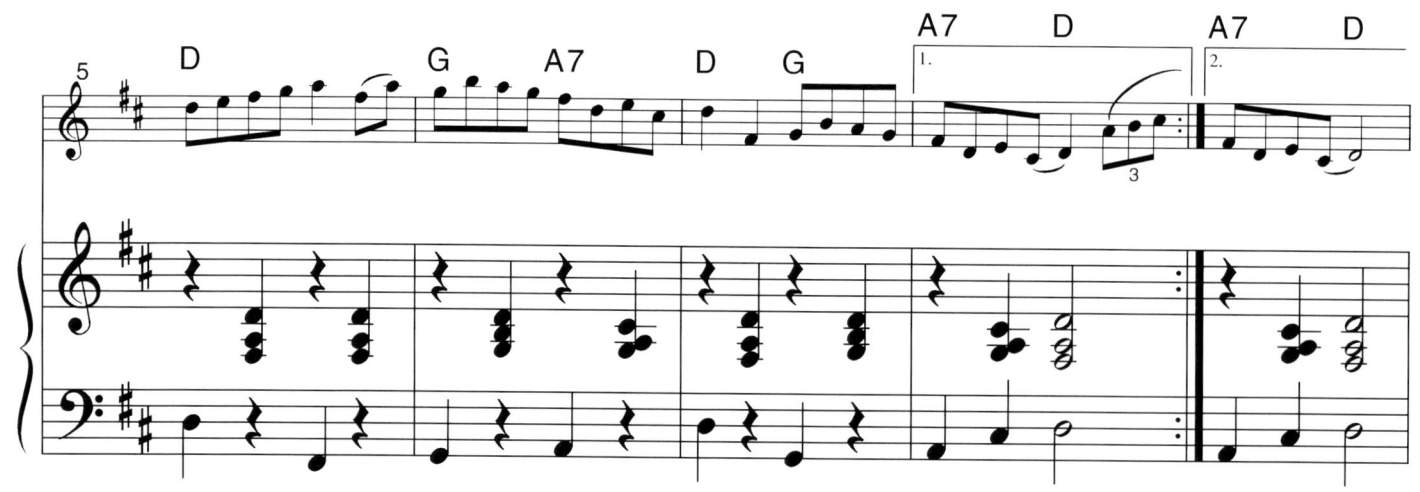

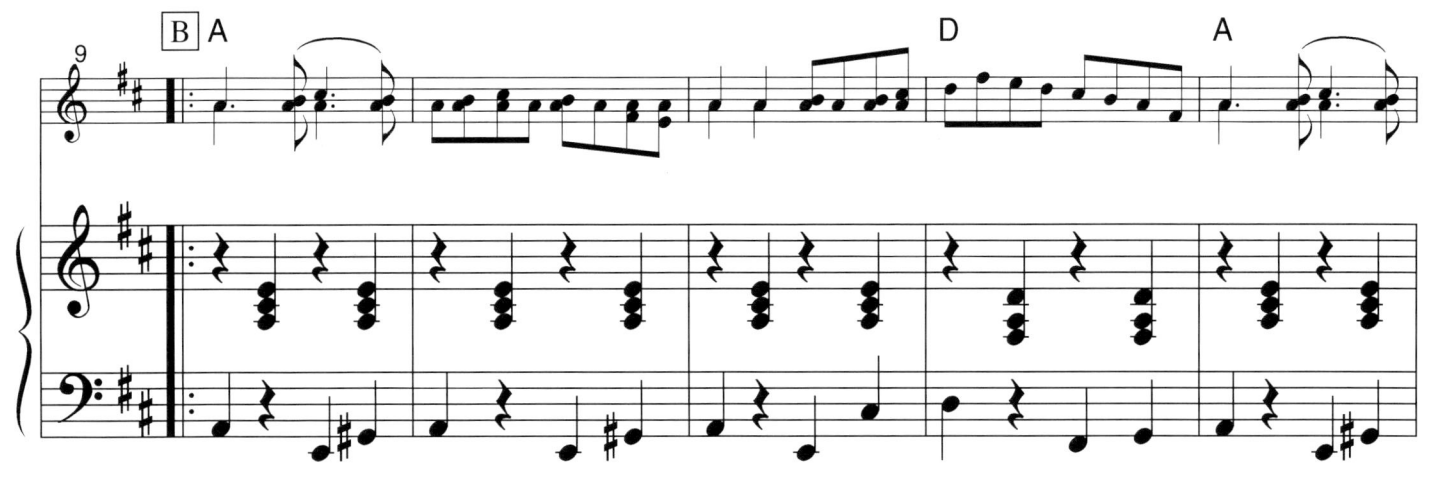
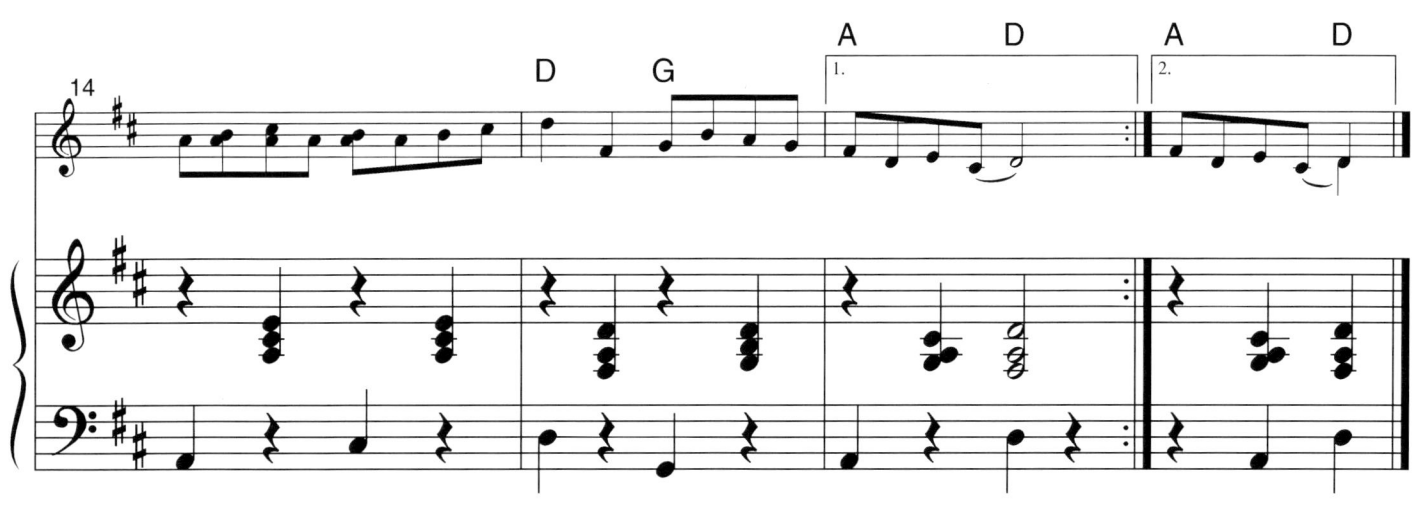

26 Jolie Blonde

This tune is so common among Cajun musicians that it has long been considered the Cajun national anthem. This tune is in the key of A and would normally end on an A chord; however, for variety, I recorded this tune ending with a D chord.

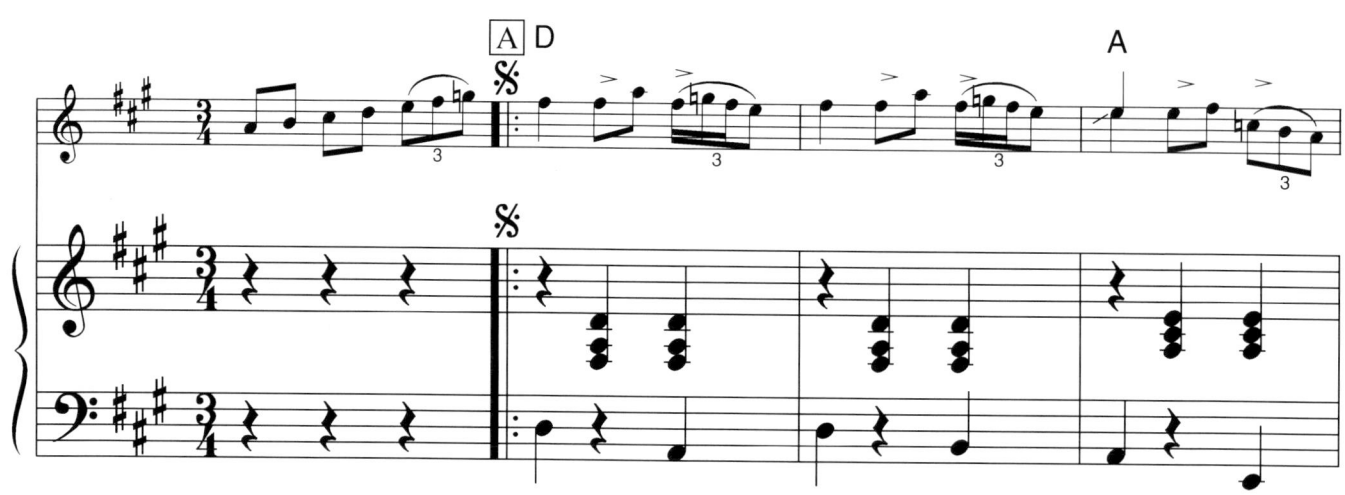

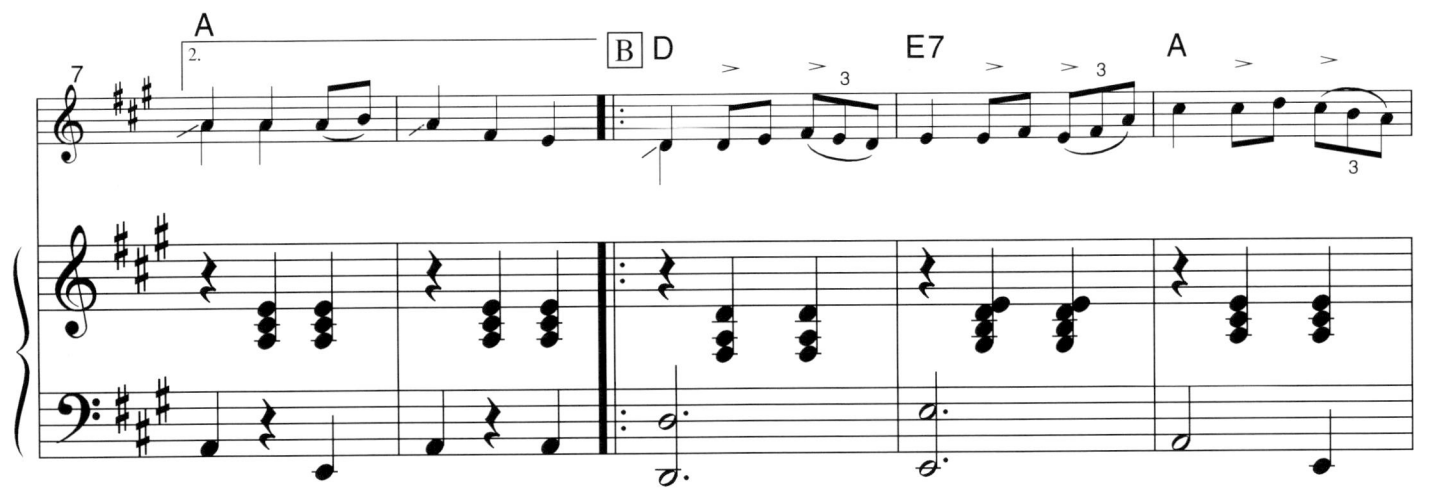
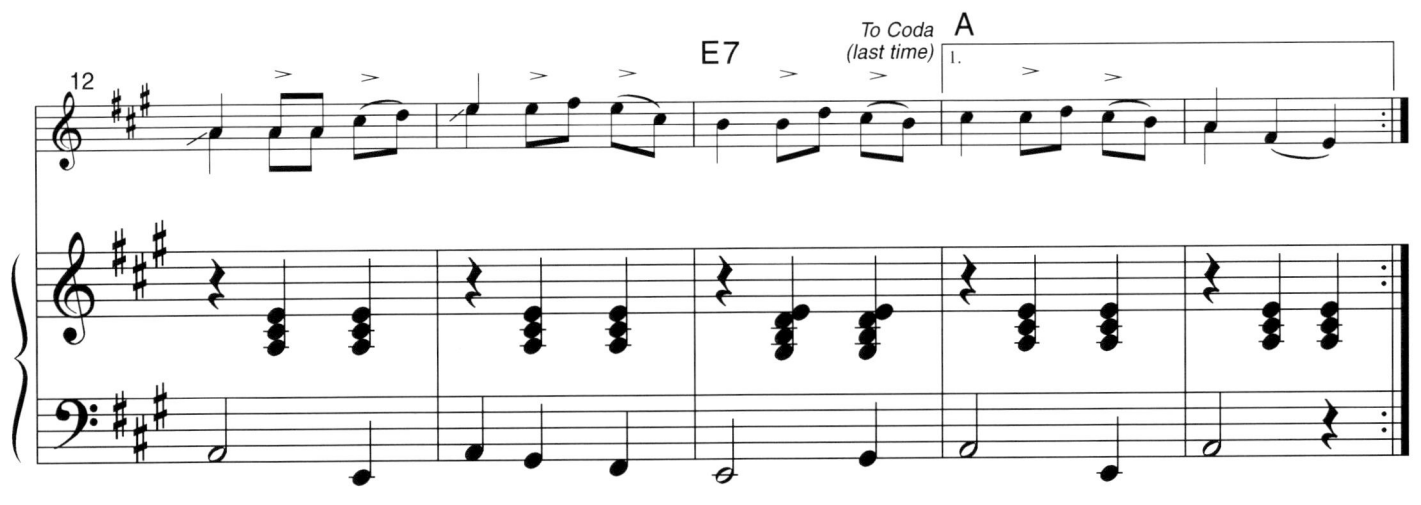
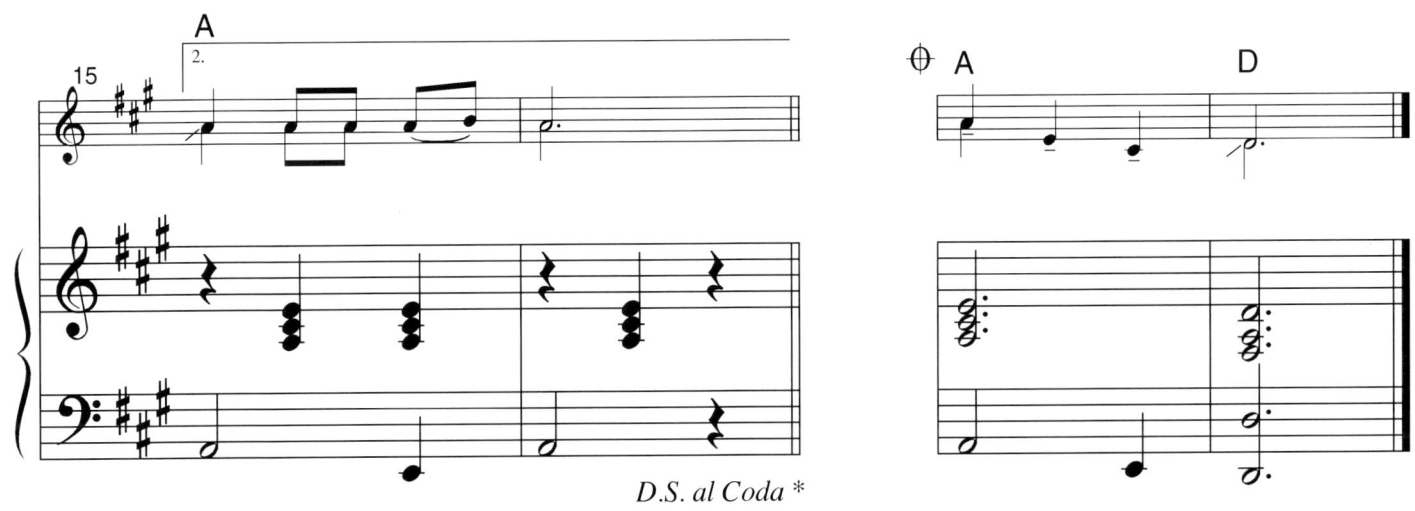

D.S. al Coda *

* Repeat A and B as desired.
Last time through B, take the coda
instead of the 2nd ending.

27 Big Walleye Blues

©Brian Wicklund, 2000, Witches Tree Publishing, BMI

This tune is named after the Minnesota state fish. It is elusive, and good eating. It's the fish anyone is happy to catch in the North Country. In this tune, a half-step slide up to the note is indicated with a / and a half-step down is \ .

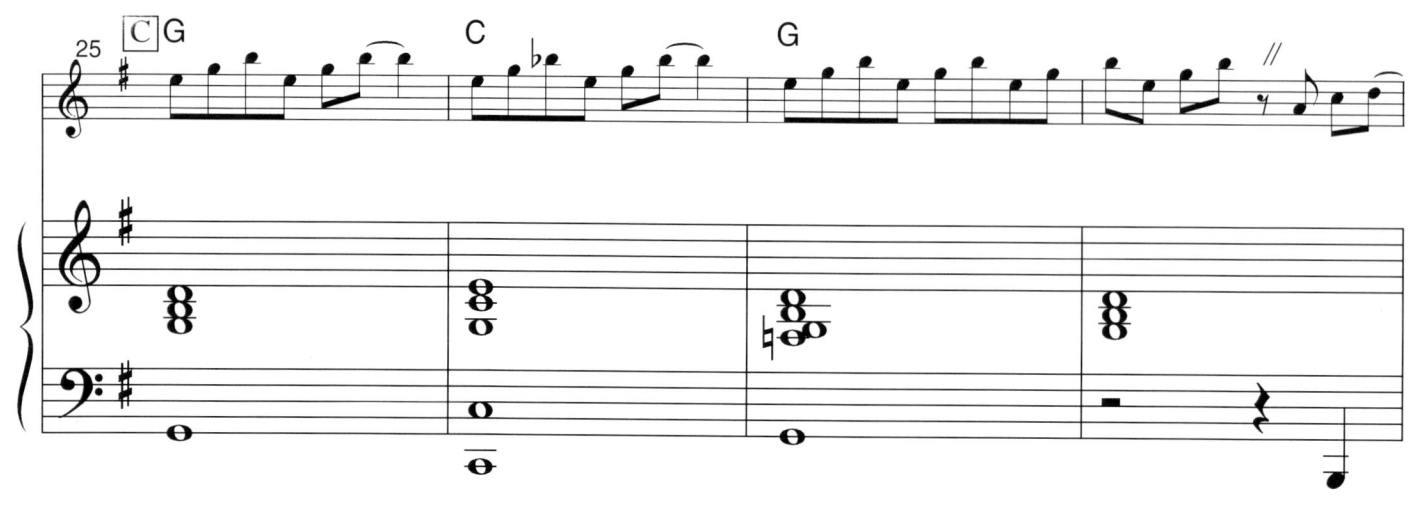

This page intentionally left blank

Piano Backup Basics

Playing backup piano with a fiddler is loads of fun! Adding the low sounds of the bass notes and the harmony notes of the chords to the melody played by the fiddle create a big, full, satisfying sound. Fiddlers from Ireland, New England, Quebec and many other places have played – and recorded – with piano players. The piano parts in this book are based in traditional backup styles going back many years. Some of the masters of piano backup you can hear on recordings include Bob McQuillen (New England), Felix Dolan (Ireland) and Gilles Losier (Quebec). Listening to these players will do more for you than any words or printed music.

As you'll see, the arrangements in these books are straightforward. In part, this is was done so they can be played with the chords published in the fiddle books in this series, and to reflect the harmonies on the accompanying CDs. On the other hand, you are not limited to the notes on the page. So for those who'd like to spice things up a bit I offer a bit of advice, and a sample arrangement that demonstrates some of piano backup's possibilities. First the advice:

"Think of yourself as a jeweler," an old piano player once told me. "The melody is the jewel and your job is to make the most beautiful setting you can." Part of making a good setting for fiddle tunes is to stay out of the way. Most fiddle tunes are centered in the octave and a half above middle C. When you're filling in harmonies, be sure to keep the chords lower than that. As a general rule, keep middle C near the middle of your chord. You can see some of the chord shapes I prefer in the arrangements in this book. As you can see from my arrangements, you can use the same chord shape over and over. Again, you don't want to steal the spotlight from your fiddler, you just want to support them! When accompanying a lower voiced instrument such as viola or cello, explore voicing your right hand chords up an octave to play above the melody.

For each volume in this series I have chosen one tune to demonstrate a few of the backup piano player's tricks of the trade. For this volume the tune is "St. Anne's Reel". Fiddle tunes are often used for dancing and many of the dances fit the music beautifully. Sometimes it's fun to help the dancers fit the dancing to the tune by emphasizing the phrasing. A basic "oom-pah" or "boom-chuck" works fine most of the time, however, in this version of St. Anne's Reel I use some rhythmic tricks to break things up and give the tune a new shape. This version also uses a diminished chord to move from the D to the E minor in measure 10, and a popular French Canadian lick in measure 12.

These are just a few ideas and more that the specifics, I hope they give you a bit of the flavor. Again, listening to the masters is the best instruction, but experimenting and stretching are part of the tradition. Whatever you do, though, remember your job as a jeweler. Good Luck!

St. Anne's Reel Variation

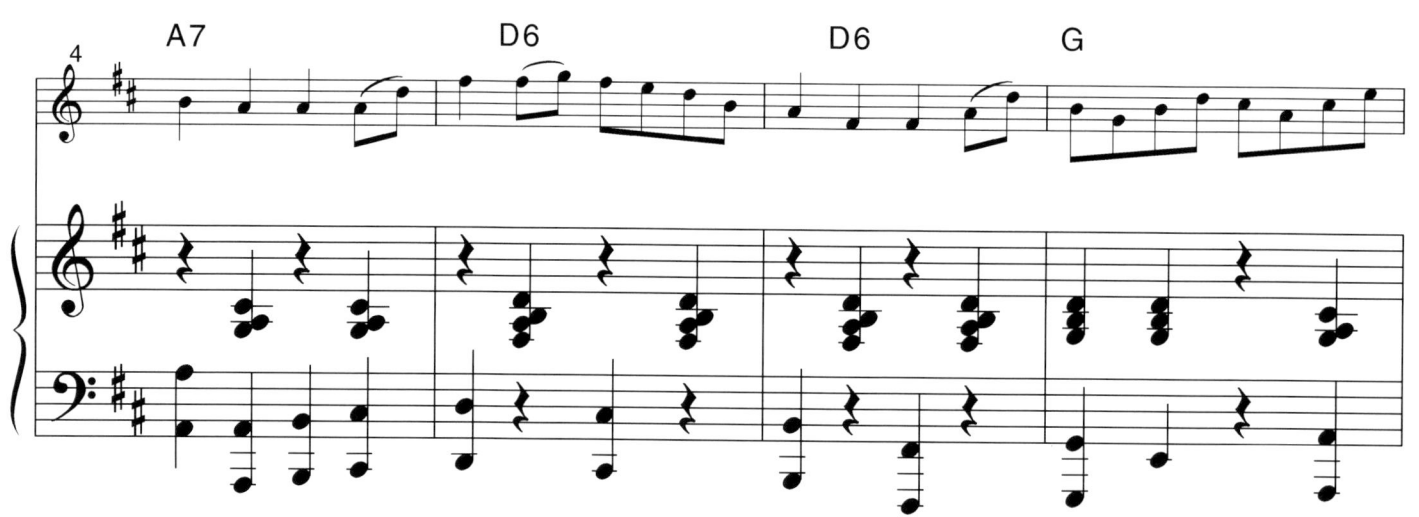

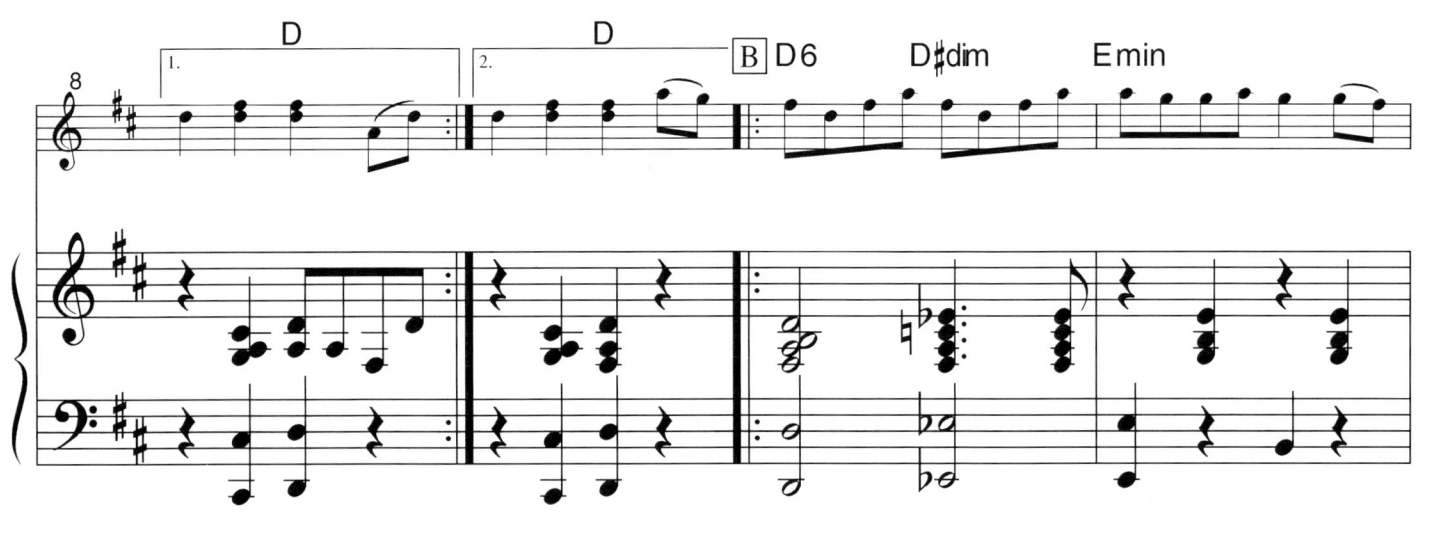

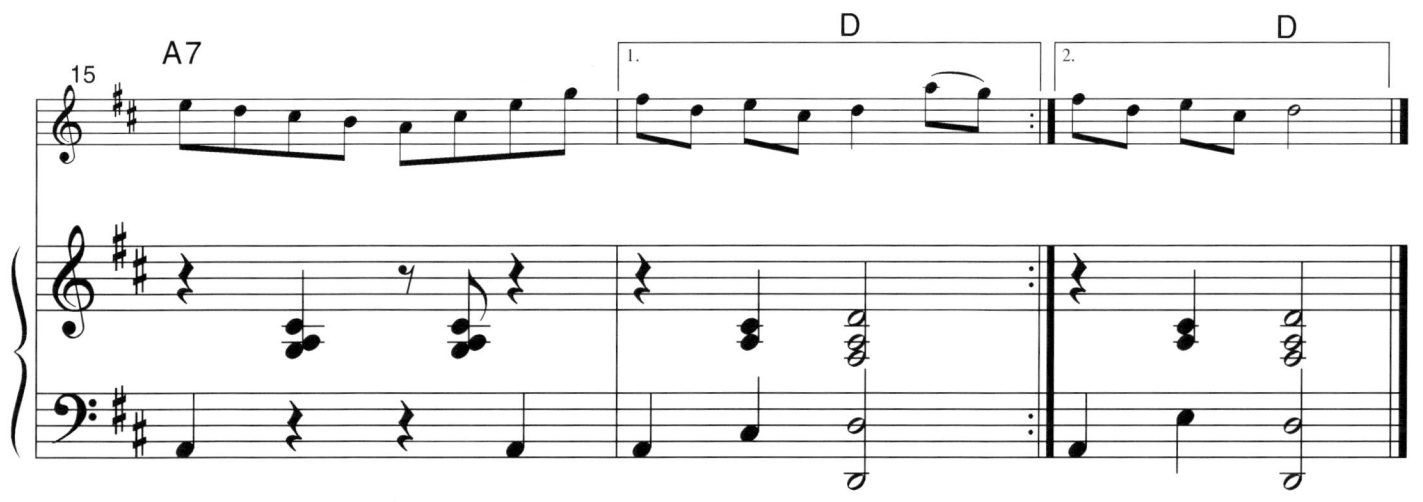

A Guide to Bluegrass Style Arranging

Bluegrass style jams differ from many other folk style jams in that rather than everyone playing the melody in unison, one person at a time plays a solo on his or her instrument. That means that when not playing a solo, musicians play backup. Below are a couple of examples of how tunes could be arranged. A jam leader can use this as a guide for getting started.

	Fiddle	**Mandolin**	**Banjo**	**Guitar**	**Bass**
1st time	**Intro / Solo**	Chunk	Rolls	Strum	Bass line
2nd time	Chunk	**Solo**	Chunk	Strum	Bass line
3rd time	Long bow	Chunk	**Solo**	Strum	Bass line
4th time	Chunk	Chunk	Rolls	**Solo**	Bass line
5th time	**Solo / ending**	Chunk	Rolls	Strum	Bass line

Here's another possibility:

	Fiddle	**Cello**	**Viola**	**Piano**	**Bass**
1st time	**Intro / Solo**	Long bow	Chunk	Back up	Bass line
2nd time	Chunk	**Solo**	Long bow	Back up	Bass line
3rd time	Long bow	Chunk	**Solo**	Back up	Bass line
4th time	Chunk	Slap	Long bow	**Solo**	Bass line
5th time	**Solo / ending**	**Solo / ending**	**Solo / ending**	Back up	Bass line

And, a possible arrangement to a song with singing:

Vocal	Fiddle	Cello	Viola	Piano	Bass
	Intro / Solo	Long bow	Chunk	Back up	Bass line
Verse 1	Long bow	Chunk	Long bow	Back up	Bass line
Chorus	Long bow	Chunk	Long bow	Back up	Bass line
	Chunk	**Solo**	Long bow	Back up	Bass line
Verse 2	Long bow	Long bow	Chunk	Back up	Bass line
Chorus	Long bow	Long bow	Chunk	Back up	Bass line
	Long bow	Chunk	**Solo**	Back up	Bass line
Verse 3	Chunk	Chunk	Long bow	Back up	Bass line
Chorus	Chunk	Chunk	Long bow	Back up	Bass line
	Long bow	Chunk	Chunk	**Solo**	Bass line
Verse 4	Long bow	Slap	Long bow	Back up	Bass line
Chorus	Long bow	Slap	Long bow	Back up	Bass line
	Chunk	Long bow	Chunk	Back up	**Solo**
Chorus	Chunk	Long bow	Chunk	Back up	Bass line

Use this chart to make your own arrangement

The publisher gives permission to photocopy this page.